A BIBLE STUDY GUIDE

Praying WITH WOMEN OF THE BIBLE

FOR 30 DAYS

SHERRY HARNEY

HarperChristian Resources

Praying with Women of the Bible for 30 Days

Published in Grand Rapids, Michigan, by HarperChristian Resources. HarperChristian Resources is a registered trademark of HarperCollins Christian Publishing, Inc.

Requests for information should be sent to customercare@harpercollins.com.

ISBN 978-0-310-17159-1 (softcover)

ISBN 978-0-310-17182-9 (ebook)

HarperChristian Resources titles may be purchased in bulk for church, business, fundraising, or ministry use. For information, please e-mail ResourceSpecialist@ChurchSource.com.

First Printing April 2025 / Printed in the United States of America

CONTENTS

INTRODUCTION

A WALK ALONG THE OCEAN WITH JESUS AND HANNAH

Two thousand miles is a long way! I grew up in Holland, Michigan, and by God's grace we had the joy of serving a church and raising our three sons in a neighboring city a short distance from my childhood home. My parents were able to be engaged with our family, most of my childhood friends still lived in the area, and for a decade and a half my husband and I served a loving and healthy local church just thirty minutes from Holland.

LIFE WAS GOOD

Then, everything began to change. One by one, our boys grew into young men and headed off to college. Los Angeles, Chicago, and a university in Michigan became home for Zach, Josh, and Nate, respectively. I missed them more than I could have imagined. Thankfully, I had the stability and security of hundreds of relationships built over a lifetime, and all of them were just across town or a short drive away.

UNTIL EVERYTHING CHANGED

God's call came with clarity, and both my husband, Kevin, and I knew what we had to do. We packed our belongings, our life, and our hearts and moved them all two thousand miles away to Monterey, California. The people at our new church were loving and sweet, and new friendships were forged. The West Coast was beautiful.

AND I WAS STILL LONELY

I sensed the Holy Spirit directing me to read Psalm 23 at the start of every day. I obeyed this spiritual nudging, which gave me some spiritual encouragement and perspective. But there was still a growing ache deep in my soul. In the past I had faced heartache, just like every human being does in life, but I had never experienced this kind of loss. It descended like a dark cloud, and I could not seem to pull out of it. I did not have the skills needed to climb out of the pit I was descending into.

About three months into this difficult season, I knew something needed to change as the trajectory of my emotional life took a downward turn. Since I grew up in the church and loved the Bible, I looked for a friend who understood pain, sorrow, and long-term discouragement. The Holy Spirit brought Hannah to mind. Sure, she lived millennia before me, but I was drawn to her journey of suffering. I read her story, as told in the book of 1 Samuel, and decided I needed to devote some time to meditating on her journey of pain and honest communication with God. After doing that, I knew I had to come before the Lord, like Hannah, and be brutally honest with how I felt.

I decided to take a walk along the coast. Just me, Jesus, and Hannah's story. There is a walking trail weaving for mile after mile between the Pacific Coast Highway and the ocean. I decided in my heart to walk until something happened in my soul.

I needed help. I was desperate.

Have you ever been there?

Are you there today?

As I walked, I talked with Jesus. I meditated on Hannah's struggle, so deep she had no words but only groans. I was not tracking time, but after walking for several miles, praying and groaning to God, I ran into a couple of women along the trail. They were providing water for people doing a training run for an upcoming marathon along that very route. They were kind and friendly, and we struck up a conversation. I had no idea that the Holy Spirit had placed them there to add their voices to the ministry that Jesus and Hannah were doing in my heart.

These two women were so kind that I shared some of my story with them and why I was on this long walk that was now paralleling the people training for the marathon. I told them of the recent move and how much I missed my family, friends, and old life in Michigan. They listened intently and then probed a bit. "How old are your boys?" I told them and explained that they were scattered at three different schools in three different states, and none of them lived in Monterey with us.

Both women had very knowing looks on their faces. It turns out that each of them had gone through the empty-nesting process and had experienced similar loss and emotions. They validated my pain and assured me that most moms experience similar struggles in this unique season.

My sorrow did not instantly disappear. But as I turned around and began the walk back to my car, I sensed I was also making an emotional and spiritual turn toward hope. These ladies were part of the answer to my prayer. I had no idea that this was one of the primary sources of my struggle. They gave me clarity and hope I would get through it. Like Hannah, I became aware that there were real and valid reasons for the lament of my heart. Like Hannah, I had cried out to God from the depths with wordless groans. Like Hannah, I knew that God heard my prayer and brought me to a place to have this conversation with these two ladies.

When I reached my car, I realized my walk ended up being several miles of communion with my Savior and two sisters I now knew better than I had before that journey along the coast. God used Hannah's faith and story to give me the courage to be honest with God and present my prayer need with groans because I didn't know how to pray in all the confusion of this changing time in my life.

WALKING AND PRAYING WITH WOMEN OF THE BIBLE

The thirty lessons contained in this book are each as unique as the women whose stories they tell. This is not meant to be an academic study of women in the Bible, but you will certainly learn from the Holy Spirit–inspired accounts of women who met God in real and personal ways. This is not meant to be a traditional Bible study, but you will learn from the scriptural records of real women who talked to the God who made them.

My prayer is that you will engage with each woman as a friend. Someone you could take a walk with and learn from. I hope after each lesson that you feel like you have started a new relationship with a woman you will meet one day in glory. If you find yourself taking a walk with Jesus and Sarah, or Jesus and Elizabeth, or Jesus and Martha, this book will be the blessing I am praying God desires it to be.

THE PATH AHEAD: ENGAGING IN THE JOURNEY

Each woman who reads this study is beautifully unique and your spiritual journey is just that . . . yours! In the same way, every woman in the Bible has her own story. Their encounters with God are like a rare pearl that has its own shape and shine. As you immerse yourself in the prayer experiences of these women, invite God to speak to you. Glean lessons that ignite your heart and enliven your imagination.

The vision of this study is for you to meet women from the pages of Scripture. To become more familiar with how prayer fit into their lives. To hear their voices lifted up in praise, calling out in pain, thanking God for his goodness, confessing brokenness, crying out for help, and so much more. Then, to see your prayer life expand and take on new and glorious depth, texture, and power.

THE STRUCTURE OF EACH SESSION

To accomplish this vision and engage on a deep level with each biblical woman, we will do three things in each session of this study guide.

1. We will look at **Her Need**. With each scriptural woman, we will take time to get to know her as deeply as the biblical text and the leading of the Holy Spirit will allow. We will identify an area of need, struggle, challenge, or joy that she experienced. Some of the things that will give us a window into her story and soul will be her name (in the ancient world names often revealed a great deal about a person), her world and life context, some of her unique characteristics, and, of course, the biblical account.

   In some cases, the prayer will be overt and recorded plainly in the biblical text. In other cases, we will focus on the woman's life situation and what she may have been praying about. Finally, some of the women have an implied prayer with only groaning, tears, shouts of joy, or some other expression. In these cases, we will do our best to extrapolate her prayer with great attention to the biblical setting and with awareness of the way our hearts respond in specific life settings. With all of these women, we will seek to learn from their encounter with God in the flow of real life, from the depths of sorrow to the heights of joy.

2. We will take time to think about **My Need**. We will identify two or three lessons from each woman's journey and take time to reflect on how these specific experiences of an ancient sister can relate to our spiritual journey. You will have time to think, ponder, question, grapple, rejoice, and delight in where you are in your prayer journey.

3. In the third and final part of each session, we will think about **Our Prayer**. We will take a walk with each woman as we grow in prayer. You will find prayer exercises you can personalize and contextualize for your life. Each session will have prayer experiences that grow out of the heart and soul of the woman we learned from.

This simple structure will give you a focused look at the life of each woman and how prayer brought God near to them. In addition, it will help you take what you learn and instill it into your journey of faith and prayer.

MY JOURNEY OF PRAYER

I love to read and have a wonderful library of books on prayer, spiritual formation, education, evangelism, and other topics that stir my soul. One thing I like to do is learn a little about the author. In some cases, I have had the privilege of meeting and getting to know the person who wrote the book, and this gives me a fresh perspective on what I am reading. With this in mind, I'd like to introduce myself and let you know a little about my journey.

I grew up in a home where talking with God was woven into the fabric of our daily family life. My journey of prayer began as far back into the recesses of my memory as I can go. There was a chorus we sang in church that I loved as a child. It painted a picture of intimacy with God that I carry with me to this day. The hymn, written by Charles Austin Miles, is called "In the Garden." Here are the words of the chorus that captured my young heart:

> . . . ***I come to the garden alone,***
> *While the dew is still on roses;*
> *And the voice I hear, falling on my ear,*
> *The Son of God discloses.*
>
> . . . ***And He walks with me, and He talks with me,***
> *And He tells me I am His own,*
> *And the joy we share as we tarry there,*
> *None other has ever known* (emphasis added).[1]

This picture of intimacy with my Maker and of natural conversation with God is one that has guided me through the ups and downs of life. Prayer has been a foundation of my life through every season.

My prayer life has grown as I have walked with my husband, Kevin, for over forty years of marriage. Through the amazing highs and surprising lows, we have called out to God, listened for God, expressed our sorrow, and lifted up our praise as a couple. One by one, God provided us three sons: Zach, Josh, and Nate. I have watched them grow into men, marry godly wives, and now we have five grandchildren and five grand dogs. I pray for my sons, their wives, and the grandchildren every day. One of my greatest delights is that almost every week one of my sons or one of their wives will reach out and ask for prayer. We pray together often.

By God's kind grace, I have been able to write two in-depth studies about women in the Bible: *Twelve Women of the Bible* and *Twelve More Women of the Bible*. These were written in partnership with video studies taught by women such as Lysa TerKeurst, Lisa Harper, Bianca Juarez Olthoff, and Chrystal Evans Hurst, among others. In addition, I have had the honor of writing the book *Organic Prayer: Discover the Presence and Power of God in the Everyday*.

---

1 C. Austin Miles, "In the Garden," Hymnary, 1912, https://hymnary.org/text/i_come_to_the_garden_alone.

It is a biblical study on prayer and a collection of lessons and practices that help people lead a life immersed in communication with God.

In this thirty-day study, *Praying with Women of the Bible*, I have been intentional to focus on the stories of women in the Bible and how we can learn to pray from their life experiences. My voice, as a writer, is minimized in this book so that you can hear the stories, sorrows, joys, voices, and prayers of amazing women who walked in faith long before any of us were born. My prayer is that, as you meet them, you will be led to fresh, powerful, and life-changing places of conversation and intimacy with the God who made you and loves you. If someday, in this life or in glory, we get to meet, I would be honored to hear your stories of faith and prayer.

May you walk with him, talk with him, and hear the Lord of Glory whisper to your heart, *You are my own.* May the Holy Spirit help you encounter the God of heaven and his Son Jesus in unique and joyful ways as you walk with him and talk with him.

With you on the journey,

Sherry Harney

LESSON 1

EVE

Praying When Temptation Is Near

GENESIS 3:1–20;
2 CORINTHIANS 11:3

HER NEED

MEETING EVE

Eve began her life in perfect paradise. Harmony was the norm. Sin had not yet descended on the human family. But temptation was still slithering through the land and looking for someone to entice. What do you do when the enemy dangles a tasty morsel in front of you, and everything inside of you wants to take a big bite? We have all been there.

Eve's name derives from the Hebrew word for life, and it likely means something like "life-giver," or "mother of us all." She was made by the very hands of God, and her life was a staggering collection of "firsts." She was the first woman God spoke to as well as the first woman who spoke to God. She was the first woman with no history of sin. Eve was the first wife, the first mother, and the first mom to lose a child. She was also the first woman to face Satan's enticing temptation and the first to give in to his lies. As we all know, she would not be the last.

READ: GENESIS 3:1–20; 2 CORINTHIANS 11:3

REFLECT

> *Then the LORD God said to the woman, "What is this you have done?" The woman said, "The serpent deceived me, and I ate."*
>
> **—Genesis 3:13**

HER STORY

Prayer is being with the God who made us and communing with him. Prayer is both speaking to our Maker and also listening to his voice. The sense of Genesis 3 is that Adam and Eve had a pattern of walking and communing with God in the cool of the garden. Eve experienced face-to-face, perfect communication with her Maker. She lived a life of intimate prayer with God. What an incomprehensible gift!

At some point, God had given clear instructions and boundaries to Adam and Eve. Read these words from her conversation with the enemy: "The woman said to the serpent, 'We may eat fruit from the trees in the garden, but God did say, "You must not eat fruit from the tree that is in the middle of the garden, and you must not touch it, or you will die"'" (Genesis 3:2–3). Loving boundaries and a clear warning—God speaks those to all of his children.

After Adam and Eve disobeyed God's boundaries and sin entered the world, everything changed. When God showed up the next time (in Genesis 3:8), he had a few questions for Adam and Eve. God knew they were hiding and avoiding contact because they had stepped into the enemy's trap. They had swallowed the lure of the serpent and were hooked.

Adam and Eve were not walking with God. They were not listening to his voice. They were not talking to him. Any time we shift from talking with God to listening to the enemy of our soul, we are headed for trouble.

Do you see what happened to Eve? It is the same folly the enemy tries to entice us to embrace: Stop talking with God. Converse with Satan. This might sound a bit dramatic, but it is absolutely what Satan still does. When we start debating what God has said (in his Word and by his Holy Spirit) the battle is already halfway lost. We are in grave danger when we stop talking with God and miss the opportunity to meditate on his words.

After God called out Adam and Eve and they emerged from their hiding, we read of God's specific conversation with Eve: "What is this you have done?" (Genesis 3:13). Every one of us knows the feeling of being caught and called out. It might have been when you were a little girl, a young teenager, or just last week. When we are caught, like Eve, the temptation is to cover one sin with another.

RATIONALIZATION. BLAME. FINGER-POINTING. LIES.

The final words that God spoke to Eve in this heartbreaking drama were honest declarations of what consequences would mark the life of Eve (and women through history). Eve's story teaches us to make communication with our Maker a priority. This was her need, and it is ours. When temptation comes, pray. Don't turn from God but talk with him.

MY NEED

Eve was living in paradise, and temptation still came her way. Every woman who seeks to walk with Jesus knows that the enemy is still whispering lies and dangling the poisoned fruit of enticement to sin right in front of us. We all know the bitter results of taking that first bite. We also know the peace and joy that come when we turn to God, seek his power, talk with our Savior, and say no to temptation.

- When does the enemy most often seek to tempt you and draw you from the path of Jesus? Identify the common tactic of the enemy and be ready to call out to God in these moments.

- Think of a time you felt Satan's lure and ask God to help you identify the ways the enemy seeks to deceive you.

- How are you setting aside time and space to communicate with your Maker in ways that grow intimacy with God and strengthen you to stand strong against the enemy?

LESSONS FROM EVE

1. **Cry out to God in times of need.** When we need help, when the enemy entices us, when Satan whispers or shouts lies, we need to call out to God and draw near him. Eve failed to do this but learned that God is always near; even when we run the other way, he draws near and finds us.

2. **Block your ears to the enemy.** Satan is a master manipulator and an experienced enticer. When we hear the sinister lies of the enemy, we need to plug our ears, talk more with God, fill our minds with Scripture, and find healthy believers to talk with and pray with.

3. **Learn to recognize the lies and deceit of the enemy.** One of Satan's best skills is camouflage. He does not want us to be aware of what he is up to and how he is seeking to destroy our lives. The apostle Paul writes these words in his second letter to the church in the city of Corinth, "But I am afraid that just as Eve was deceived by the serpent's cunning, your minds may somehow be led astray from your sincere and pure devotion to Christ" (11:3). Make a point of identifying the most common ways he tries to lure you in, and then fortify yourself in advance to stand against his ploys and walk in pure devotion to Jesus.

MY REFLECTIONS

What is God teaching me about prayer through Eve?

1. When God is speaking to you (through the Bible, by his Spirit, through a person, or some other way), how do you know it is your Creator speaking? What do you do to test and make sure you are hearing from God?
2. What are ways you can intentionally and consistently block your ears and heart from the lies, lures, and enticements of Satan?
3. Look back on your life and recall a time when you were so closely connected with your Maker that the enemy couldn't even get your attention. Describe that experience below.

OUR PRAYER

HONEST AND HUMBLE CONFESSION

When we fall into sin, we are all prone to run and hide from God. It is always best to run to God and confess. Take time to read Psalm 51, a powerful prayer of confession. Then, write your own prayer of confession.

IDENTIFY AND FORTIFY

Ask God to show you two or three areas of your life where you tend to get tempted when you are not connected with your Maker. Write them down here or in your heart.

- ____________________
- ____________________
- ____________________

Lift up each of these areas of temptation in passionate prayer and ask God for eyes to see when you are being tempted, courage to fight back, and wisdom to run to God in these soul-challenging moments.

PRAYER ECHOES

Learn from your sister Eve. Remember her story, both the good and the bad. Ask God to help you close your ears to the lies of the enemy and open your heart to the love, power, and grace of Jesus.

LESSON 2

HAGAR

Praying to the God Who Sees Me

GENESIS 16

HER NEED

MEETING HAGAR

Unnoticed, unimportant, unseen. Many women have moments when they feel this way, and Hagar was no exception. She was of Egyptian descent, and her name might mean "flight" or "fugitive." When you come to know her story, you'll discover how fitting her name was.

Hagar was enslaved. The Bible does not affirm slavery, although in the ancient world (and sadly in parts of the world today) it was common. God hates oppression and is always seeking to care for the marginalized, and so should his people today. In Hagar's world, polygamy (a man having more than one wife) was common. It was also common for enslaved women to have the role of childbearing in their households. The fact that characters in the Bible adopted this practice is not an affirmation that it was right. Our focus is not to dissect the confusing-looking practices of people in the ancient world but to gain insight from Hagar's prayer in the midst of her broken life and culture.

Though she was marginalized, Hagar was the first person in the Bible to see an angel. God chose a foreigner, a female slave, to encounter the one true living God. She may have been mistreated by others, but God showed up and showed mercy to this hurting woman. She seemed to be a pawn on the chessboard of Abram and Sarai's lives, but she was seen and valued by God.

READ: GENESIS 16

REFLECT

> *She gave this name to the Lord who spoke to her: "You are the God who sees me," for she said, "I have now seen the One who sees me."*
>
> **—Genesis 16:13**

HER STORY

God shows up in our difficult times. The Lord of heaven cares for us even when others treat us poorly. Hagar learned what we all need to recognize: Even when no one else seems to see us or care about our needs, our Maker knows us, sees us, and loves us.

To understand the story of Hagar, we need a snapshot of how she was connected to Sarai (Sarah). God had promised Abram (Abraham) and Sarai descendants like the stars of the sky, even though they did not yet have any sons or daughters (Genesis 15:5). So, Sarai decided to run ahead of God's plan. At Sarai's suggestion and prompting, Abram agreed to marry Hagar (a woman enslaved in their household) and seek to have children with her. This led to immediate conflict when Hagar became pregnant. Chaos descended on the family. Hagar could read the writing on the wall and knew Sarai did not want her around. She did what her name meant. She fled for the hills.

At this point, through a heavenly messenger, God spoke to Hagar. The conversation (paraphrased below) was honest and direct.

Angel: Where are you going? (Genesis 16:8)

Hagar: I'm running from my home and from Sarai. (Genesis 16:8)

Angel: Go back home. God's promise of many descendants is still true. You will have a son! (Genesis 16:9-12)

What happened next is a tender lesson to people of every generation until Jesus comes again. Hagar gives God a name. In this prayer interaction, a broken, fugitive, praying woman identifies the character of God.

Hagar: You are the God who sees me. (Genesis 16:13)

How true. How personal. How needed. In a world where so many feel invisible, forgotten, or simply overlooked, this is a powerful reminder! In her prayer, Hagar has one more thing to say.

Hagar: I have now seen the One who sees me. (Genesis 16:13)

What joy this must have breathed into the suffocating fugitive Hagar! She went back to Abram. Her son Ishmael was born. And her story continued.

MY NEED

Am I seen? Valued? Cherished?

In a world that has devalued almost everything, it is easy to think that we don't matter. In a time when celebrities and influencers have a voice but most of us do not, we can feel unheard and unseen. Yet the God who came to Hagar also let her know she was seen and valued. Hagar comes to us and declares the same message.

- Do you live each day aware that the Maker of the universe has his eyes firmly fixed on you?

- Are you confident that you are precious in God's sight and the apple of his eye?

If you take a slow and thoughtful walk with Hagar, you will discover that the God you worship sees you, and you can see him. God fills your need to be seen.

LESSONS FROM HAGAR

1. **Suffering can open our eyes and heart to God.** The God we worship and serve does not cause or celebrate evil. Suffering is not his invention. But our God draws near when we are in pain and facing sorrow. It is in these times that we often see him more clearly. Don't forget to search for God even in the midst of those daunting moments of life.

2. **People may not see us, but God always does.** We all have times when we feel like Hagar. The world feels like it is spinning out of control, and in your pain you feel alone. No one sees you. No one understands. No one cares. But like Hagar, we need to learn that God sees us.

3. **God sees us, and we can see him.** It is easy to imagine that God sees us. He is God after all—of course he sees us. What is unique in Hagar's prayerful declaration is that she saw God! It is valuable to go through every day remembering that God sees you, and you can see him too. Keep your eyes open for "God-sightings."

MY REFLECTIONS

How can lessons from Hagar's journey of faith impact my life?

1. What is a part of your life that is messy right now? How can you invite God to show up and be near you in your need?

2. When was a time that you were going through pain and suffering of some kind (relational, physical, financial, spiritual, emotional, or some other kind of suffering)? How did you experience God more profoundly during this time, and how did you see his face more clearly?

3. How will your outlook on life change if you live each day convicted that God sees you at all times?

OUR PRAYER

YOU SEE ME WHEN . . .

Think through a normal day. What do you do? Where do you go? Make a list of a few seemingly insignificant experiences of your life.

- ____________________
- ____________________

- ____
- ____
- ____

Read each one out loud and then declare, "God, you see me in this moment of my day, help me see you!"

OPEN MY EARS AND MY EYES

Hagar saw the God who saw her. Sometimes we face significant struggles and feel alone. We might even run from God, from the church, and from family and friends. Mental health challenges, illness, marriage conflicts, frustrations at work, children who stray from us and the Lord—all of these can prompt us to isolate ourselves from God and our support systems. Write a prayer asking God to help you know that he is with you as you pray for help in any areas of struggle you are facing right now.

PRAYER ECHOES

In her pain, loneliness, and fear, Hagar encountered God. She declared the name of God based on what she experienced with him. He was the God who saw her! Join Hagar in this prayer as you look on the One who loves you in the messes of life—the God who sees you and who shows up right where you are.

LESSON 3

SARAH

Impossible Prayers

GENESIS 18:1–15; 21:1–7; HEBREWS 11:11

HER NEED

MEETING SARAH

How do you hold onto faith in a situation that seems hopeless? How do you pray when every human instinct tells you that there is no way the answer will be yes? What do you do when you have lifted up the same prayer for weeks, months, or even years, but heaven seems silent? Is there hope for women who have become hopeless when it comes to a very specific and painful prayer? I would suggest you take a walk with Sarah.

Sarah was the only woman in the Bible whom God renamed. God changed her name from Sarai to Sarah. What an honor! When God gave her the name Sarah, he also called her "the mother of nations." This is a very interesting title because she had been praying to become a mom for a very, very long time but was still barren (Genesis 17:15–16). Let's be honest. This can be a painful story for those who cannot bear children, so we proceed with care in Sarah's story.

Sarah wasn't perfect, and her treatment of Hagar was sinful. Nevertheless, she was a woman of tenacious and unyielding faith. God has always blessed imperfect people, and Sarah is no exception. She encountered moments when she needed God to fortify her soul and grow her faith. We all do! Even when the odds were against her, she trusted that God would one day hear her prayers and give her a child. She believed in God's provision and power but also laughed at the thought of God's promise being fulfilled in the later years of her life.

READ: GENESIS 18:1–15; 21:1–7; HEBREWS 11:11

REFLECT

Now the LORD was gracious to Sarah as he had said, and the LORD did for Sarah what he had promised.

—Genesis 21:1

HER STORY

God had given his promises to Abraham and Sarah . . . and God always keeps his promises, right? Earlier in Genesis God promised Abraham, "I will make you into a great nation" (12:2). God also promised him, "To your offspring I will give this land" (12:7). The Creator of heaven also spoke to Abraham and Sarah about a future where their family members would be so numerous that they would outnumber the stars of the heavens (Genesis 15:5). There was just one big and baffling issue facing this rapidly aging couple: They had no children.

This would lead to a crisis of faith for anyone. You want to believe, but every human indicator says there is no way this is happening. For Sarah, the test of faith was about starting a family. It could be a different crisis with you or me.

With God's promises in her mind and genuine faith in her heart, she prayed. Try to imagine Sarah in her twenties asking God for a son or daughter, but pregnancy eluded her and Abraham. Sarah's faith stayed strong as she prayed into her thirties as she watched all the other women she knew starting families. As she prayed into her forties, she likely watched her neighbors' children become teenagers and grow toward adulthood. With faith and tears, Sarah prayed into her fifties and sixties as her friend's children had their own children, and yet she remained barren. You and I know that Sarah would have faced piercing pain and struggles on this journey.

The flames of trust in God might have flickered a bit, but they were not extinguished. Even when she was well past the normal "childbearing age" (Hebrews 11:11), Sarah remembered God's promises and believed that Yahweh was faithful and would certainly accomplish his will, albeit in his timing. As Sarah walked through her seventies and eighties, against all hope, she believed, trusted, and prayed for the promise of God to be fulfilled. But she also struggled.

Here is an interesting little biblical nugget. Sarah is the only female adult whose age we are given in the whole Old Testament. And it makes sense. After nine decades of living on planet Earth, it was finally time for her to have a baby. That's right, her husband, Abraham, was one hundred years old, and Sarah was ninety. The news of Sarah's pregnancy was so shocking and surprising that when Abraham got word that she would have a child, he literally fell down laughing (Genesis 17:17). When God sent messengers to reinforce this shocking reality, Sarah also laughed. Hers was more of a chuckle to herself as she pondered exactly how this would work and look to her neighbors (Genesis 18:12).

Nine months later, their world changed . . . and so did ours! Read the following words slowly and joyfully from God's Word:

Now the Lord was gracious to Sarah as he had said, and the Lord did for Sarah what he had promised. Sarah became pregnant and bore a son to Abraham in his old age, at the very time God had promised him. Abraham gave the name Isaac to the son Sarah bore him.

—Genesis 21:1–3

It must have seemed impossible to Sarah that she could conceive after decades of barrenness. Impossible to keep praying in faith when all evidence (from a human perspective) indicated it would never happen. Impossible for this couple to begin a family when the number of candles on their birthday cake would look like a small forest fire.

When you walk with Sarah, you learn from a woman who struggled but never stopped believing and praying. Her son, the fulfillment of God's promise, had a very interesting name. His name was Isaac, which means "one who laughs or rejoices." What a perfect name to put an exclamation point on the end of decades of prayer!

MY NEED

What is your impossible prayer? Where have you given up? Where is your faith waning? Why keep praying when your tears have dried up and your faith is being tested? Sarah's story is not meant to teach us that if we pray long enough, we will always get heaven to bend to our requests. But Sarah's story does challenge every one of us to keep praying no matter what.

- Pause and remember a time when God answered a prayer that you lifted up for a very long time. What did you learn on this journey?

- What is a prayer you keep bringing to the throne of God but have not yet received an answer (other than wait, which is an answer)?

LESSONS FROM SARAH

1. **Never stop believing and praying.** Let's be honest. We can get distracted or discouraged and stop praying after days or weeks. Heaven stays silent for a month, and we figure it is time to move on to some other prayer need. Don't lose faith, and don't stop knocking on the door of heaven. Remember how Sarah is lifted up in the biblical list of faithful people, "And by faith even Sarah, who was past childbearing age, was enabled to bear children because she considered him faithful who had made the promise" (Hebrews 11:11).
2. **God loves doing the impossible.** It was Jesus who said, "With man this is impossible, but with God all things are possible" (Matthew 19:26). Let the story of Sarah boost your faith and remind you that the one who spoke and all the heavens came into existence is the same one who hears each prayer you lift through tears, sorrow, laughter, and joy.
3. **God's timing rarely lines up with ours.** If Sarah had her way, she would have conceived as a young woman and walked that journey along with her friends. But God does not work on our timeline. On the contrary, he often moves at a pace that we don't understand. Don't forget that God's wonderful plan may be far different than our own plans.

MY REFLECTIONS

How can lessons from Sarah's journey of faith impact my life?

1. What is a prayer you gave up on a month, year, or decade ago? In light of Sarah's story, how could you return to that prayer in faith?

2. What was a seemingly impossible prayer that you lifted up at some point in your life that God answered? How did God's amazing answer spur you on to other prayers of faithful trust?

3. How have you experienced God answering a prayer you lifted up in a way you did not expect or with timing that was different than you would have wanted?

OUR PRAYER

REIGNITE MY HEART

Take time to write out a prayer asking God to rekindle your heart to pray for things you have grown weary of lifting up to him.

STORIES OF ANSWERED PRAYER

Reach out to two or three women whose faith you respect. Ask each one to tell you a story of answered prayer that truly surprised them. Write a few words to describe the story and write down one prayer lesson from each story.

Story 1: ____________________

____

____

Lesson: ____________________

____

____

Story 2: ____________________

____

____

Lesson: ____________________

____

____

Story 3: ____________________

____

____

Lesson: ____________________

____

____

PRAYER ECHOES

- It all comes down to grace.
- God answers prayer—a gift of grace.
- Our Maker delays saying yes to a prayer we lift up—God's wise grace.
- The Lord of the universe fulfills his promise—a reminder that he is eternally gracious.

LESSON 4

REBEKAH

Praying Through Family Conflict

GENESIS 25:21–34; 27

HER NEED

MEETING REBEKAH

Being in the midst of intense relational conflict can drive us to prayer. When that tension is inside the walls of our own home, it is even more urgent. When Isaac's wife, Rebekah, gave birth to twin boys, you would have thought all her dreams would have come true, right? However, the strife between these brothers would become a familial conflict of epic proportions, one that would have driven her to prayer.

As Rebekah's boys grew up and life became complex and competitive, we can be confident that her prayer life grew right along with her family. Esau, the firstborn son, was an outdoorsman who loved hunting and was close to his father, Isaac. Jacob, the second out of the womb, was far less rugged than Esau. He tended toward indoor activities and connected most naturally with his mother. Jacob also turned out to have a deceptive streak that kept popping up through much of his life. No one has perfect children, and Rebekah learned this reality up close and personal.

How do you pray through sibling conflict? How do you seek God for help in your marriage when there is tension in the home? What do you cry out to God when you can't mend broken family relationships and your family is becoming a cauldron of conflict rather than a place of peace? Let's walk with Rebekah and learn how to pray for a family in turmoil.

READ: GENESIS 25:21–34; 27

REFLECT

> *The Lord said to her,*
>
> *"Two nations are in your womb, and two peoples from within you will be separated; one people will be stronger than the other, and the older will serve the younger."*
>
> **—Genesis 25:23**

HER STORY

Not days and weeks of sibling conflict but years and decades—that was Rebekah's reality. She became one of the biblical matriarchs when she married Isaac. She was under God's covenant and blessing that began with Abraham and Sarah, and she knew the prophecy that "thousands upon thousands" of descendants that would come from her family line (Genesis 24:60). Rebekah would have learned that her family was part of God's plan to bless every nation of people in the whole world. How hard could this be?

You might think that Rebekah would experience parental smooth sailing and that her kids would be models of kindness and faith. Well, guess again. In Genesis 25:22–23 we get a preview of what Rebekah would experience:

> *The babies jostled each other within her, and she said, "Why is this happening to me?" So she went to inquire of the Lord. The Lord said to her, "Two nations are in your womb, and two peoples from within you will be separated; one people will be stronger than the other, and the older will serve the younger."*

We have all heard the term *sibling rivalry*. Esau and Jacob took this to a whole new level. There came a point where Jacob literally moved out of the house and the country. Why? Because his brother Esau was ready to kill him. How does a mother pray at a time like this? What happens in a mother's heart when one of her sons is away from the family for almost two decades? Imagine the prayers of Rebekah through those years and the joy she experienced when her sons were finally reconciled.

As a mother who cherished her children, Rebekah would have prayed with hope, tears, and faith. She would have gone deep in prayer for the conflict that continually erupted between her twin sons. She would have lifted up the prayer of every mother navigating sibling conflict and tension: *God of heaven, bring your peace to our family, reconciliation between the children, and hope into a situation that feels hopeless.*

Rebekah's prayers were lifted up not just for days, weeks, months, or years. They were declared over and over for decades. She spent decades in persistent and faithful prayer, with many of her prayers going unanswered within her lifetime. Through all the turmoil and trials, God *did* answer her. Rebekah and Isaac conceived after twenty years of trying. Jacob finally came home after twenty years of being away from home. There was peace between the brothers after a lifetime of conflict. And the promise to Abraham was fulfilled in the Messiah through the family line of Isaac and Jacob (Luke 3:34). Yes, it took time. There were bumps along the road. But God ultimately used Rebekah's prayers for her family to bless the whole world.

MY NEED

Every believing mother prays for her children; it comes quite naturally. The need for prayer often comes spontaneously: "God help me!" "Grant me heavenly wisdom." "Please make them stop!" "Keep my kids safe." "Give me strength to love them well." These and many other prayers pour from a mother's lips and heart. You get the picture.

Not every woman who learns this lesson from Rebekah will get married or be a mom, but we all have family ties and connections. We all have moments when we taste the bitter tears that come when conflict descends on a family. We can all learn to pray as we listen to Rebekah's story.

- Where is there conflict in your family, and how can you pray for God's peace to calm the relational storms?

- Are there ways you can cry out to heaven on behalf of your family?

LESSONS FROM REBEKAH

1. **God's timing is not our timing.** God hears our prayers, but sometimes the answer comes after a significant time of waiting. Ask God, through his Holy Spirit in you, to grow you in patience.
2. **We are all a mixed bag of good and struggles.** Rebekah's life was filled with victory, faith, and patience. It was also marked by favoritism, deception, and division. It should give us hope to see great people in the Bible who were still very human. We should build on our strengths and also cry out to God for help to overcome our weaknesses.
3. **Answered prayers can look different than we imagine.** Even when our prayers are answered, there is no guarantee that everything will go smoothly. Keep praying!

MY REFLECTIONS

How can lessons from Rebekah's journey of faith impact my life?

1. When was a time that, like Rebekah, God's timing and your timing did not come close to aligning? What did you learn about prayer and God through this experience?

2. What is a prayer you lifted up for a long time, but you stopped praying (intentionally or accidentally)? How can you reignite a passionate prayer for this specific area of your life (or the life of someone you care about)?

OUR PRAYER

PRAYING SCRIPTURE

In John 17 (the entire chapter is an account of the longest recorded prayer of Jesus) our Lord prayed for all of those who would one day come to faith through the ongoing ministry of his disciples. In part of the prayer, the central focus of Jesus was unity among his people. Read this portion of Jesus' prayer slowly and embrace it as your own.

> *My prayer is not for them [the disciples] alone. I pray also for those who will believe in me through their message [that's us], that all of them* ***may be one****, Father, just as you are in me and I am in you. May they also be in us so that the world may believe that you have sent me. I have given them the glory that you gave me, that* ***they may be one*** *as we are one—I in them and you in me—so that they may be brought to* ***complete unity****. Then the world will know that you sent me and have loved them even as you have loved me.*
>
> **—John 17:20–23** (emphasis added)

Use this prayer of Jesus to guide you as you intercede for your family.

WRITE IT OUT

Take time to write out a prayer for the restoration of broken relationships guided by the life of Rebekah. Lift up people in your family who are in conflict with each other or with the whole family.

PRAYER ECHOES

Rebekah prayed with a patient and believing heart for decades. Learn from her example. Don't give up! Keep seeking the face of God even when you feel exhausted and at the end of your energy and ability. God is faithful!

LESSON 5

LEAH

Praying When Life Feels Unfair

GENESIS 29:16–35

HER NEED

MEETING LEAH

She wanted to feel loved. She longed to be cherished. If only she could be seen as first in her husband's eyes and life, but she knew she was second at best. Leah's story is one of longing for love and experiencing misery, hungering to feel connected but knowing she was detached and overlooked.

Her deepest hunger was to know that she was valued and important. She did not find it in her marriage. Even bearing children did not fully fill the chasm in her heart. Leah walked a road that many women travel. Her heart cried out to be loved, but the circumstances of her life made her feel unnoticed.

Ultimately, she discovered that God was her rock, her hope, and the one who was worthy of her praise. No matter what life brought her way, she could cling to this rock-solid reality. She was loved by God, and his eyes were on her. Leah learned that there are times in life when this has to be enough!

READ: GENESIS 29:16–35

REFLECT

> *When the Lord saw that Leah was not loved, he enabled her to conceive.*
>
> **—Genesis 29:31**

HER STORY

As you took time to read the text of Genesis 29:16–35 and heard this portion of Leah's story, you were certainly shocked and probably saddened, and if you felt what she really experienced, you may have shed a few tears. Leah longed for love. She just wanted her husband to look at her with delight and desire in his eyes. Instead, she felt forgotten and rejected year after long, painful year.

Women living in our day and generation have a very hard time comprehending Leah's world: Multiple wives (sometimes even sisters) sharing the same husband. Female servants bearing children for their mistress. Arranged marriages that included a payment for a bride. It all seems so ancient and primitive.

In Leah's day, names carried deep and powerful significance, and this was certainly the case with her first four sons. Because she knew that Rachel (her little sister) had Jacob's attention and affection, Leah hoped that providing a son would be the breakthrough her heart desired. Maybe if she bore Jacob a boy to carry on the family name, he would finally love her. We gain a window into Leah's life and emotional journey through the birth and names of these sons.

Reuben is born first. His name in Hebrew means "behold, a son." We read in Genesis 29 that Leah is feeling two things as she names her first boy. First, she recognizes that she is so miserable that even God in heaven must see it. Second, she hopes that her husband will finally love her. In the naming of Reuben, Leah reflects on being unloved and miserable.

Simeon comes second. His name derives from the Hebrew verb "to hear." Leah declares that she is confident God has listened to her and given her a second son as an act of grace, because even the Maker of heaven has heard that she is not loved. Can you feel her pain? Even with a son in each arm, she is still longing for a love not yet received.

Levi was born on the heels of Simeon, and his name comes from the Hebrew verb "to attach." Leah expresses the hunger of her heart to feel attached to Jacob, her husband. Even after a wedding and the birth of two sons, she feels disconnected and far from him. Sadly, Levi's birth does not seem to forge the bond with her husband that her heart yearns for.

Judah, boy number four, is born next. Did you notice what Leah declares as he is named? His name sounds much like the Hebrew verb "to praise," and this connects to the words that burst from the still-broken heart of Leah. She no longer laments feeling unloved. She does not focus on being unnoticed. She does not talk about wanting to feel connected to Jacob. Now Leah turns her eyes and cries to heaven and says, "This time I will praise the LORD" (Genesis 29:35).

Leah's needs were not met by her husband, Jacob. Her soul was not satisfied by having one, two, three, or four sons. But finally, after the birth of Judah, she looks to the Lord of heaven and decides to lift up praise right where she is.

MY NEED

Have you been there? Longing to be loved? Desiring to be connected? Hungering to be first in the eyes and affection of the person who means the most to you? In those moments when our longings are not satisfied and our dreams are not realized, we can take a walk with a sister named Leah. She lived there for many hard and painful years. She has a story to tell us and lessons to share. Have you ever felt that your dreams and longings for a man who makes you feel whole might not be realized in the way you had hoped? If so, you are in good company. Even those who have a great marriage learn that no man can fully satisfy what their heart longs for.

- If you have children, you have learned that being a mother can fill deep longings, but it does not fill all of the yearnings of our soul. And sometimes it even leads to times of worry, sorrow, and pain.

- When your heart is broken by the disappointments of life, one of the best responses is to fix your eyes on Jesus, recognize his presence, and lift whatever praise you can muster up.

LESSONS FROM LEAH

1. **Through our pain, praise can still ring out.** Even through tears and loneliness, Leah decided to lift her praise to God. This is a lesson for every generation. We can't control a husband or children or anyone for that matter, but we can choose to worship and praise God through whatever we face.

2. **Every married woman will face disappointment.** Leah had a husband who worked hard and provided for a large family. She did her part and (in her culture and time) worked hard to be a great wife. Yet, her relationship with Jacob never had the intimacy and closeness that her heart desired and needed. There were things she wanted from her marriage that Leah never received. At any given moment, this can be true of any marriage. Don't forget that even the best relationships can experience moments of frustration or despair.

3. **Having children brings joy but does not meet our deepest needs.** Leah did exactly what she knew Jacob wanted. In her world, sons who carry on the family name meant far more than they do today. So she had a son, and another, and another, and one more for good measure. Sadly, this did not bond her to Jacob or satisfy her own heart. Mothers in every generation discover that there is joy in having and raising children, but there are longings that this does not satisfy. Remember that there is joy beyond that which comes from parenthood, and be sure to seek out those other joys in your life as well.

MY REFLECTIONS

What is God teaching me about prayer through Leah's story?

1. What are the places in your heart where pain exists because longings are unmet and dreams are not fulfilled?

2. What is an area of your life that you need to grow in trust of God's sovereign will, even when you don't understand it?

3. How can you choose to lift up praise and worship to God when you are feeling pain, loss, and loneliness?

OUR PRAYER

PRAYING THE PSALMS

It has been said that some portions of Scripture teach us to pray, but the psalms pray for us. Take time to lift up the following portion of Psalm 10. Pray it out loud and let this be a springboard to move you into honest and heartfelt prayer:

> *But you, God, see the trouble of the afflicted; you consider their grief and take it in hand. The victims commit themselves to you; you are the helper of the fatherless. . . . You, Lord, hear the desire of the afflicted; you encourage them, and you listen to their cry.*
>
> **—Psalm 10:14, 17**

WALKING WITH ANOTHER WOMAN

Who is a woman in your life that is going through deep personal pain (maybe in a marriage, or as a mother, or perhaps longing to be a mother but not yet able to conceive)? Begin praying for this woman on a regular basis. Then, reach out and ask if there are specific ways you can be praying for her. As you are able, get with her for a time of face-to-face prayer.

PRAYER ECHOES

Even though Leah's marriage seemed to stay tough and her family life was far from perfect, her decision to praise God through the pain is an example for women of every age. And one glorious part of her legacy is this: Through the family line of her fourth son, the Lion of the Tribe of Judah, the Messiah, Jesus our Savior, came to the earth.

LESSON 6

MIRIAM

Praising God After Suffering

EXODUS 2:1–10; 15:1–21

HER NEED

MEETING MIRIAM

She was born into slavery, forced labor, and oppression. Life was so hard that singing, dancing, and lifting prayers of praise to God were not the norm in this season of Israel's history. Miriam must have wondered: *Will I ever sing with joy and freedom again*?

Throughout most of her life, even in her earliest childhood memories, Miriam saw, felt, and experienced things that no little girl should have to face. Unfortunately, girls and women today still have difficult and even traumatic experiences that they should never have to face. For any woman who is on the long road of healing from struggle and needs to see light at the end of this seemingly endless tunnel, take a walk with Miriam. For anyone who wants to help a friend along the way, take a walk with Miriam as well. She has a story to share.

READ: EXODUS 2:1–10; 15:1–21

REFLECT

Then Miriam the prophet, Aaron's sister, took a timbrel in her hand, and all the women followed her, with timbrels and dancing. Miriam sang to them:

"Sing to the Lord,
for he is highly exalted.
Both horse and driver
he has hurled into the sea."

—Exodus 15:20–21

HER STORY

Miriam was the sister of Aaron and Moses, two of Israel's leaders. She was identified as a prophetic leader. She displayed courage from her youngest days. On top of all this, she was inspired to write a song expressing praise to God that we can read in the pages of Scripture. Our insight into the life of this strong sister comes in two primary scenes: one from her childhood and one many years later.

Scene 1: Miriam as a young girl. In Exodus 2, Miriam appears as a little girl who is introduced to evil and suffering at a painfully young age. She sees the babies of friends and neighbors being thrown into the Nile River and drowned because Pharaoh, the Egyptian king, is terrified of the growing number of Hebrews in his land. The King of Egypt sees this nation as a potential military threat growing right in his own population.

In the face of evil, Miriam is courageous and clever. She attentively watches the small basket where her mother placed her baby brother, Moses. It floats in the reeds at the edge of the great river. Then Miriam sees Pharaoh's daughter, a young woman, go to that very spot and see the baby. Instead of executing Moses, the princess has compassion and decides to raise him as her own. Thinking quickly, Miriam cleverly makes an offer to Pharaoh's daughter: "Shall I go and get one of the Hebrew women to nurse the baby for you?" Pharaoh's daughter replies, "Yes, go." Miriam then goes and fetches her mother (Exodus 2:7–8). If you missed the irony of what just happened, please read it again. Miriam runs and brings her (and Moses') mother to the riverside. Pharaoh's daughter offers to pay Moses' mother to help raise Moses. God is sovereignly guiding the life of Moses and using Miriam in his divine plan.

The interlude between Scene 1 and Scene 2 is many years of pain, oppression, and conflict that threatens to steal all joy from life.

Scene 2: Miriam as a faithful and godly woman. In Exodus 15 we meet Miriam again several decades later. She is there when the people are being delivered from captivity in Egypt. Immediately after they have miraculously crossed the Red Sea, Moses leads the people in a song of victory. Then, Miriam joins in. As a prophetess among the people and a respected leader, she adds instrumentation (timbrels, much like a modern tambourine) to the praise and introduces dancing. She even adds her own verse to the prayerful song that mirrors the spirit of what was already happening in worship. She and all the women sing, dance, and celebrate God's power and victory. This is a scene of mourning turned to dancing!

MY NEED

Will I ever sing again? Will there be light at the end of the tunnel I am traveling through? Can I find hope along the way? Miriam never lost her faith even through decades of slavery and oppression. She clung to her God, and so should we. She served God's purposes, and so should we. She kept a song locked away in her heart, and so can we.

- Where are you feeling bound, trapped, or stuck?

- Are you able to hold to your faith and trust in God in the middle of the long and dark tunnels of life that we all travel?

- When you pass through the sea of chaos and come out on the other side, are you ready to sing, dance, and celebrate God's deliverance?

LESSONS FROM MIRIAM

1. **Invite others into prayer.** Miriam was a charismatic leader who swept other women into deeper places of praise. They followed her example and cried out to God with song, prayer, instrument, and dance. Ask the Lord to use you to help other people come near him and engage in deeper places of worship. Even in the hard seasons, God shows up and brings victory.

2. **Join with others in prayer and song.** One of the blessings of praying in community is listening to the prayers of others and agreeing with them as we lift a hearty "Amen!" We can also add to their prayers and expand on them, and this is exactly what Miriam and all the women were doing. When you gather with believers to seek the face of God together, listen closely to their prayers, songs, and worship and build upon what you hear. Remember that in your times of victory, others are still in the tunnel of pain. Be sure to pray with them right where they are.

MY REFLECTIONS

What is God teaching me about prayer through Miriam?

1. What are some characteristics of God that can lead you to praise and worship him in the hard times of life and in the moments of victory?

2. What are ways that prayer and worship become richer and more meaningful when we join with others in seeking the face of our God in the middle of our struggles?

3. Miriam was an example of taking others into deeper places of prayer and worship. Who is a person God has placed in your life that is in the tunnel of sorrow, and how can you encourage this person to stand strong?

OUR PRAYER

WILL YOU PRAY WITH ME?

God calls us to live in community. We need each other. In the moments of captivity, bondage, and oppression, Miriam needed others and so do we. It takes courage to ask others to lift us up and support us in prayer. Write down the names of some people you love, trust, and know would pray for you in a hard season.

- ______________________________
- ______________________________
- ______________________________
- ______________________________

Keep this list handy and when you are in the tunnel of pain. Reach out and ask these people to pray with you. Keep them updated on how you are doing so they can pray specifically for your needs.

MAY I PRAY WITH YOU?

Keep your ears and eyes open; you will see people in need. When you do, offer to pray with them right there and then.

You will also see people in a time of celebration. Ask if you can join them in praise. You may even be able to lift a song in praise to our Lord with them.

PRAYER ECHOES

Miriam joined in and sang with others. She was not a one-woman show, and the focal point was not her—it was God! Let's make sure every time we join in prayer, gather for worship, and seek God in community, we keep Jesus fully on the throne and ourselves humbly bowing down to give him glory.

LESSON 7

RAHAB

A Prayer of Searching Faith

JOSHUA 2

HER NEED

MEETING RAHAB

Afraid. Uncertain. Second-guessing so much of what she had been told and taught.

Rahab lived in a time of national uncertainty. As a Canaanite, she had heard of the massive movement of Israelites who were marching toward her city. Although her home was in Jericho, surrounded by a seemingly impenetrable wall, she was still trembling in fear along with so many others in her land because of the Israelites and Yahweh, their God. Her story begins when two men come knocking on her door, but not for the usual reasons men come to a brothel. These were spies from the enemy army descending upon her land, and they were looking for a place to hide.

Something strong was stirring in her heart as she saw these spies, even as it melted in fear. Could the God of the Israelites truly be so powerful? Could trust and faith in Yahweh fulfill her family's need for protection? We do not have a full record of what Rahab and the spies discussed, but along the way Rahab's trust and faith shifted from the idolatrous gods of Canaan to the heavenly King of Israel. Rahab loved and cared about her family and was ready to align her heart and life with a whole new people group and follow their powerful God.

READ: JOSHUA 2

REFLECT

When we heard of it, our hearts melted in fear and everyone's courage failed because of you, for the Lord your God is God in heaven above and on the earth below.

–Joshua 2:11

HER STORY

Rahab was a Canaanite prostitute who lived in the city of Jericho. Her body had probably been used by more men than she could remember, and her heart would have been hard toward the world system that had trapped her in the ancient sex trade. Rahab's soul must have felt so empty. However, into her broken life Yahweh, the Creator God, was about to enter in a dramatic way.

The two men who came to her home that day were looking for a place to hide. While in her home, as you can imagine, they told stories of the God they worshiped and followed. Yahweh had freed their people from captivity in Egypt (an ancient superpower). Their God had given them victory over mighty kings and armies as they moved toward Canaan. As Rahab reflected on the rumors of a wandering people led by a God who was said to rule over the land, the sea, and all the world, her heart began to open. As she encountered two men who reinforced all she had heard, she cast aside the

idols, Canaanite gods, and empty philosophies of her past. Rahab called out to a God she had not known and made him her God and Savior.

Rahab's proclamation became her prayer of belief: "For the LORD your God is God in heaven above and on the earth below" (Joshua 2:11). This transformed sex worker, raised in a pagan environment, became a woman of faith and followed Yahweh. We can be confident of this because she is listed in the "Hall of Fame" for biblical people of faith found in Hebrews 11.

Because of her newfound faith, Rahab and her family escaped destruction when the city of Jericho fell. She became a follower of the God of Israel. Her legacy is a fascinating one. Rahab shows up in two of the most famous lists of people in the Bible. She is found in the genealogy of Jesus the Messiah (Matthew 1:5) and in the comprehensive list of faithful people in the book of Hebrews (Hebrews 11:31). That is how our God works when anyone—and I mean anyone—cries out to him and follows him.

MY NEED

Questions and confusion, seeking and searching. That was the condition of Rahab's heart. The pain of life can lead us to question ourselves, others, and our faith. What God loves to do is answer our questions and lead us in fresh new directions that align with his will and lead to the truth. Rahab changed from a used and broken woman into a model of faith. As we walk with her, God can answer our questions and clear up our confusion.

- What are some of the big questions that are swirling around in your mind today?

- Are you confident that it is good to ask hard questions of God in prayer and talk with others about our places of confusion?

- Do you have wise and godly people in your life to talk to and pray with when you have questions (even about your faith)?

LESSONS FROM RAHAB

1. **Pray to the God who sees you through his eyes and not as the world defines you.** In both the Old and New Testaments, we are reminded that this woman of faith began as a prostitute. Why does this matter? Because who we *were* is not who we *will become* in Jesus. Remember that God does not see us as the world does.
2. **Call out to God when your heart is melting.** More than once in Joshua 2 we read about how the hearts of the people in Rahab's mighty city were melting. Fear gripped them. Let's remember that times of fear and uncertainty are a great time to reach out to God in prayer.
3. **Walk by faith and not by sight.** Rahab took a huge risk. She lived in the wall of a fortress city that could withstand a mighty attack. She knew very little about Yahweh, the God of Israel. Her faith was just that—faith without sight! The evidence of God's power came only after she surrendered to him. Think about an area in your life where you need to have such faith in God.

MY REFLECTIONS

What is God teaching me about prayer through Rahab's journey?

1. What are things God sees in you that others often miss? Why is it essential for our spiritual health that we see ourselves through God's eyes and not the lens of the world around us?

2. Rahab cried to God in her fear and anxiety. Why is this such a good time to seek the face of God?

3. Rahab had a deep need for safety, protection, guidance, and hope for the future. Where do you need God's protecting hand on your life and how can you pray for God's power on you?

OUR PRAYER

SEARCHING PRAYERS

Rahab was searching for something more. In her seeking, she encountered Yahweh and was changed for eternity. Think back on your journey to Jesus. What were your questions? How did you search? Use the space provided to write a prayer of thanks to God for leading you to his heart through your search. If you are still in a time of searching in your life, use this space to write a prayer to God, ask your questions, and seek to be open to any way he will reveal himself to you.

A PRAYER OF REFRESHMENT

Rahab's soul was dry, and she found refreshment in Yahweh, the God of heaven. All of us have times of deep longing for God. We all face seasons where we feel our soul is running dry. Pray this passage from Psalm 63:1–5. Feel free to do it out loud or silently, to sing it or whisper it, but no matter how you proclaim it, lift it from the depth of your heart!

You, God, are my God,
earnestly I seek you;
I thirst for you,
my whole being longs for you,
in a dry and parched land
where there is no water.

I have seen you in the sanctuary
and beheld your power and your glory.
Because your love is better than life,
my lips will glorify you.
I will praise you as long as I live,
and in your name I will lift up my hands.
I will be fully satisfied as with the richest of foods;
with singing lips my mouth will praise you.

PRAYER ECHOES

Rahab entered a whole new life when she dared to turn from the life she knew and embrace the God she had never met before. When you meet a person who is far from God and up to their neck in the quicksand of sin, point to Jesus and invite them to place their faith in him.

LESSON 8

DEBORAH

Praying Through Vocational Challenges

JUDGES 4–5

HER NEED

MEETING DEBORAH

It is common to have women working in virtually every profession today. Even fifty years ago, however, it would have been surprising to see women laboring in many vocational settings. Thousands of years ago, it would have been unheard of to have women working as business owners, community leaders, or soldiers.

Deborah lived in the time of the judges. This period in Israel's history came right after the people entered the promised land under Joshua's leadership and before the United Kingdom of Israel was led by kings Saul, David, and Solomon.

Like a lot of working women today, Deborah wore a lot of hats. She was a wife. She was a leader in the community and helped people navigate questions, conflicts, and community tensions. She had a prophetic gift and ministered on a spiritual level among the people. Deborah also gave consultation on military matters. She served as the fourth of the twelve judges, and she was the only woman to hold this important place of leadership. She had multiple callings and would have faced challenges in all of them. Deborah needed grace and strength to navigate it all.

READ: JUDGES 4–5

REFLECT

"Hear this, you kings! Listen, you rulers!
I, even I, will sing to the Lord;
I will praise the Lord, the God of Israel, in song."

–Judges 5:3

HER STORY

Deborah was called to her job of leadership at a unique time for the people of God. During this period they went through the same cycle of behavior over and over again. Decade after decade this was the rhythm for Israel:

1. A time of peace and prosperity.
2. The leader of Israel dies.
3. The people rebel and fall into sin.
4. God removes his hand of protection.
5. There is a time of attack and oppression by an enemy.
6. The people repent and cry out to God for help.

7. God raises up a dynamic military and political deliverer (a judge).
8. There is victory and a new time of peace.

This heart-breaking pattern was in full swing when God called Deborah to rise up and become judge over the people. In a world dominated by men, Deborah stood out as a beautiful example of strength, leadership, collaboration, and humility. The judges were political, military, and sometimes spiritual leaders called by God for a season of repentance, revival, and revolution.

Into a raw and conflicted time, Yahweh called Deborah to step up. With spiritual maturity, the respect of the people, the ear of the military leaders, and courage in her heart, Deborah called the nation to rise up and fight back against the Canaanites. She summoned Barak, a military leader, and called him to gather ten thousand soldiers to drive out their enemies. He listened and agreed to fight the Lord's battle—with one condition. He wanted Deborah at his side. She said yes.

We can imagine Deborah would have prayed through every part of her amazing calling. The Old Testament records one of those prayers that Deborah lifted up in song. When the victory was won, when the people were free, when the enemy was crushed, and when a new chapter of God's blessing began, Deborah prayed. With passion and piercing honesty, Deborah and Barak lifted up a duet. A prayer put to music. A raw song of victory!

MY NEED

Some women reading these words work multiple jobs, have a variety of responsibilities, and wear a lot of hats. Life today can demand so much. What a gift to have Deborah's example to learn from!

- What hats do you wear, and what are your prayer practices for each area of responsibility? How can you be praying in each unique setting that God has placed you in?

- Are you in places that are challenging for a woman? How might you remember Deborah's journey and press on with grace and strength?

LESSONS FROM DEBORAH

1. **Give God the glory.** Deborah's song of praise gives God glory as it focuses on the Lord as the one who empowered Israel to conquer its enemies. Prayers that give God the glory he deserves are always pleasing to our Maker. Take the time today to offer such a prayer to God.

2. **Honor people in prayer.** Deborah did not take credit for the victory. As she sang and prayed, she honored the princes of Israel who led the way and the people who came to fight for their land, lives, and the glory of God. In our vocational world, we should celebrate those who work with us.

3. **Imprecatory prayer is raw and honest.** Some of the most shocking passages in the Bible are imprecatory prayers. These are cries to God about the injustice in the world. They are prayers against the evil of sinful people and nations. They are a passionate cry for God to wipe out sin and the wrong that is all around us. Deborah prayed like this and so can you. When there are wrongs in life and the workplace, pray for God's justice.

MY REFLECTIONS

What is God teaching me about prayer through Deborah?

1. The Lord has placed amazing people in your life today and through the years who intersect in your vocational world (this can be in the marketplace, the home, or any setting where God calls you to serve and work). Notice these people, pray for them, be thankful for them, and encourage them.

2. Think about a battle you are facing (or a battle a close friend or family member is going through). How can you ramp up your prayers for this battle and ask for God's victory?

3. What are some of the surprising and beautiful ways God has provided for you or someone you love? How does God's provision bring joy and what can you do to express thanks to God?

OUR PRAYER

GET A LITTLE IMPRECATORY

To help you dig deeper into the topic of imprecatory prayer, read one (or all three) of these passages: Psalms 5, 69, and 109. How do you feel when you read these? Why do you think God gives us examples of these raw and intense prayers? How do you feel about praying like this?

Let's give it a try. Think about a situation that is unjust, unfair, or evil in your vocational setting (wherever God has called you to work, be it in the home, an office, school, the medical field, or elsewhere). Write a prayer identifying what is unjust. Use that prayer to cry out to God to make things right, whatever it takes.

WRITE AND SING A PRAYER

Deborah's prayer in song has a very specific context that is hers alone. You have your own context too. So try writing a short poem, declaration, or song. Then try making up a little tune. Here is a simple structure that follows some of the themes of Deborah's song:

There was a struggle (enemy, battle, conflict) I faced . . .

But I still praised the Lord!

There were people God brought to help me through . . .

So I praise the Lord!

God showed up and helped us overcome the enemy . . .

So I will keep praising God!

PRAYER ECHOES

Deborah lifts up raw, honest, powerful prayer. Ask God to give you new boldness in your prayer life. Consider identifying a great evil in our world, your community, or even in your heart, and lift up an imprecatory prayer inviting God to destroy what the enemy of your soul is trying to do.

LESSON 9

RUTH

Praying When You Can't Make It on Your Own

RUTH 1; 3; 4:13–22

HER NEED

MEETING RUTH

We have all listened to toddlers declare the bold words, "I can do it by myself." When it comes to tying a shoe or using the potty chair, we hope there comes a day when kids can manage these and other basic tasks on their own. When it comes to walking through life, there is no age when we should try to do it all by ourselves. Ruth learned this critical life lesson. She needed community when her husband died, and she became a widow far too early in life. Every one of us comes to a place where we recognize our need for the people God has placed in our lives.

In the ancient world, a widow was defenseless. It is hard for us to comprehend today, but when a woman did not have a husband to protect and provide for her, she was almost always desolate. If there was a kind and generous family member who offered to help, there was a glimmer of hope. If not, widows could end up living in abject poverty because there were no social services and no governmental safety net.

Ruth was a Moabite and would have been devoted to the idolatrous deities of her people, including Chemosh, their chief god. By the time her story ends, not only does Ruth commit to stay by the side of her Israelite mother-in-law, Naomi, and marry Naomi's kinsman Boaz, but she also places her faith fully in Yahweh, the Maker of heaven and earth.

READ: RUTH 1; 3; 4:13–22

REFLECT

> *But Ruth replied, "Don't urge me to leave you or to turn back from you. Where you go I will go, and where you stay I will stay. Your people will be my people and your God my God. Where you die I will die, and there I will be buried. May the Lord deal with me, be it ever so severely, if even death separates you and me."*
>
> **—Ruth 1:16–17**

HER STORY

The story of Ruth began when an Israelite family left their home in the city of Bethlehem after a brutal famine came upon that region. Elimelech, his wife, Naomi, and their two sons relocated to Moab looking for food and relief. However, after settling in Moab, Naomi's husband died, and she was left alone with her young adult sons. Both of them married women from the land of Moab, and one of these young women was Ruth. About ten years later, both of Naomi's sons passed away, and she was left alone in a strange land with her two daughters-in-law, Orpah and Ruth.

When Naomi learned that the famine was over in Bethlehem, she planned to go home. Naomi advised her daughters-in-law to stay in their own land, and Orpah remained in Moab, but Ruth was devoted to going with Naomi and Yahweh. This is where we read the famous declaration of Ruth quoted earlier.

Ruth held on physically, relationally, and spiritually. She would not go back to her people and their gods. Somewhere in that decade of being part of Naomi's family, Ruth had met the God of Israel, and she came to know him as the living God. She had forsaken the idols of her people and their chief deity Chemosh. She was not walking alone but arm in arm with Naomi and heart to heart with God. After moving to Bethlehem, Ruth married again. She and her husband, Boaz, had a son named Obed, who appears in the genealogy of Jesus, the Messiah.

MY NEED

Our world cheers on rugged individualism and admires "self-made" people. It is easy to buy the lie that we can navigate the complexities of life all by ourselves. The truth is, God made every one of us for community. For Ruth, it was Naomi, Boaz, and God. Who is it for you? Who do you invite into your heart and life? How do you find strength on the journey of life through relationships?

- When have you tried to press through life on your own and discovered you needed community and connection with others?

- How does holding fast to God empower you when people in life are not available or when they let you down?

LESSONS FROM RUTH

1. **Everyone is welcome to follow our God.** The life and story of Ruth should remind us that God's arms are wide open to anyone and everyone. Who would have figured that a Moabite widow would end up in the lineage of the Messiah? Never write someone off just because they don't fit your preconceived notion of the kind of person who would embrace and follow the Jesus.

2. **Don't try to walk through life alone.** It never goes well when you try to go it alone. Moments of solitude are fine, but a life of isolation sets us up for disaster. Be sure to remember this when your heart feels the temptation to wander from community and fellowship with God and others.

3. **Devotion to people of deep faith can grow our faith.** Love for God is contagious. Passionate faith can rub off on others. Naomi clearly had a powerful influence on Ruth. As you and I walk in faith, we can influence others to follow Jesus with ever-increasing devotion. Think about some ways you can let your passionate faith inspire others in their own walks.

MY REFLECTIONS

What is God teaching me about life and prayer through Ruth?

1. Ruth cried out that she would follow God and the godly people he placed in her life until she died! Who are one or two people whose faith is devoted, real, and an example to you? What have you learned from these people, and how have they helped shape your life and faith? You may want to communicate in some way to one of those persons in your life to share your gratitude for the impact their life has had on you.

2. Who are people in your family, neighborhood, or social circles who might not seem very open to meeting and following Jesus? How might God use you and your authentic faith to help this person encounter the love and truth of Jesus?

3. Why are we often tempted to travel through life alone? Who can you connect with on a deeper level, and how might this relationship be a blessing to them and to you?

OUR PRAYER

PRAYING FOR FAMILY AND FRIENDS

Take time to pray for friends in two distinct ways:

1. Pray for friends or family members you already have. Write down the names of three or four relationships you deeply cherish.

- ______
- ______
- ______
- ______

Pray for each one by name. Thank God for what they mean to you. Pray for your relationship to be strong and rich. Pray for an area of need they are facing.

2. Pray for new friends. Ask God to bring new people into your life who can become friends. This might be for you, for them, or for both. Most of all, it could glorify God.

PRAYING FOR YOUR RELATIONSHIP WITH GOD

We are called to love God first and most of all (Matthew 22:37–38). Jesus teaches us to "seek first his kingdom" and let God take care of the rest (Matthew 6:33). Use the simple prompts below to guide you in praying for your relationship with Jesus.

Jesus, I thank you for loving me and saving me . . .

Lord Jesus, help me avoid distractions that keep me from following you closely . . .

Savior, forgive me for the ways I turn from you and walk out of your will . . .

Messiah, help me love you more and more each day . . .

PRAYER ECHOES

Ruth left so much behind to follow God. As you lift up prayers of devotion to God and surrender to his ways, prepare to leave some things behind so you can receive all that God has planned for you. Then, be sure you never travel through life alone.

LESSON 10

HANNAH (PART 1)

Praying When Dreams Don't Come True

1 SAMUEL 1:1–20

HER NEED

MEETING HANNAH

Unfortunately, we don't live in a fairy-tale world where little girls can wish upon a star or summon a magical godmother to make all their dreams come true. All of us at different points in life have faced the cold reality that not all our dreams come true, or at least not in the ways that we hoped they would.

The name Hannah means "favor," "grace," or "gracious." It is an interesting name for a woman who faced intense pain, struggle, and longing through years of unfulfilled dreams. Sometimes it takes more time than we think to step fully into what God has planned for us, and this was certainly the case in Hannah's story.

In the ancient world, many men had more than one wife. In Hannah's home there was her husband (Elkanah) and his second wife (Peninnah).

In 1 Samuel we learn that this was a deeply painful reality for Hannah. Her rival wife seemed to get pregnant with profound ease, and Hannah did not. To make things worse, with every child Peninnah delivered, her taunting of Hannah increased. This led to a depth of sorrow and pain hard for most people to comprehend today.

Hannah was patient and faithful. In all of her pain, she kept praying. She still believed in God enough to pound on the door of heaven through her tears and agony. She was also expressive and honest in her prayer life. She did not sugarcoat her prayers or hide her tears. She told God exactly what she was feeling. Hannah also told others if they were willing to listen.

READ: 1 SAMUEL 1:1–20

REFLECT

In her deep anguish Hannah prayed to the Lord, weeping bitterly.

—1 Samuel 1:10

HER STORY

Emotional pain and crushed dreams, over time, can lead a person to resent and reject God. Hannah endured year after year of indescribable disappointment. She was unable to conceive a child, and her rival wife, Peninnah, would not give her a moment of peace. It is truly amazing to read her story and see what she did and also what Hannah refused to do.

Hannah cried out to the Lord day and night. Often, when a prayer is not answered in a few days, a month, or a year, we simply stop praying. Not

Hannah! She may have been asking God to open her womb and give her a son for a decade or even longer. What a relentless spirit!

Hannah's closed womb did not close her heart. Instead, she kept drawing near to God with prayers, moans, and cries for help. Her pain did not drive her from God but caused her to draw near her Savior. Instead of burying her sorrow, she entrusted her deepest pain to the only one who could help her.

Sometimes, long seasons of suffering lead us to numb our pain in any way we can. It is a survival tactic. But Hannah did not take the easy way out and suppress her sorrow. She expressed bitter pain to God with piercing honesty. When Eli the priest witnessed her praying in the house of the Lord, he accused her of being drunk, Hannah replied, "I am a woman who is deeply troubled. I have not been drinking wine or beer; I was pouring out my soul to the Lord. Do not take your servant for a wicked woman; I have been praying here out of my great anguish and grief" (1 Samuel 1:15–16). Hannah was not intoxicated with alcohol; she was drowning and drunk with sorrow.

MY NEED

You might have dreams that no one knows. Secret longings that friends and family have never heard, but you still hide them in your heart. Maybe your dreams are public, and many people are praying with you as you strive for their fulfillment. Whatever the case, learn from Hannah. She brought her longings to the Lord and cried out for help. Sometimes, she had no words, so she groaned her heart to heaven and trusted God to interpret.

- In your moments of inward groaning or outward crying to God, do you know that he hears you? Are you confident that he still cares, even when your dreams go unfulfilled?

▶ Some dreams are just childish longings that you eventually let go of (and wisely so). Other dreams are from the Lord, and you should keep praying for his fulfillment. What dreams should you pray for more than you do?

LESSONS FROM HANNAH

1. **Sometimes people can be cruel—keep praying.** Hannah's rival was merciless and persistently cruel. Through her pain, she kept praying for God's hand in her life. When people intentionally or accidentally pound on your heart, keep asking for God to comfort and deliver you.

2. **Sometimes words that are intended to help actually hurt—keep praying.** Did you notice when Hannah's husband made an effort to comfort her when she was at a desperately low point? "Her husband Elkanah would say to her, 'Hannah, why are you weeping? Why don't you eat? Why are you downhearted? Don't I mean more to you than ten sons?" (1 Samuel 1:8). Every person who goes through a long season of pain has faced well-meaning people who try to bring comfort, but it hurts more than helps. Ask God to give you his gracious touch and pray for patience with those people whose words don't really help.

3. **Sometimes godly leaders don't get it—keep praying.** As a final spiritual slap in the face, the great prophet Eli rebuked Hannah and accused her of being drunk in the house of the Lord first thing in the morning. If someone misunderstands your pain, speak the truth as Hannah did and keep praying.

MY REFLECTIONS

What is God teaching me about prayer through Hannah?

1. What was a time you walked through a season of pain, loss, or struggle that you did not ask for or deserve? How did this season impact your prayer life and relationship with Jesus?

2. What was a time when a person treated you in a way that was painful and unfair? How did God sustain you and lead you through this time?

3. The longer the sorrow and pain last, the more we are tempted to stop praying. How can your prayers actually deepen and become richer through extended times of struggle?

OUR PRAYER

PLACING YOUR DREAMS ON THE ALTAR

Describe two dreams you carry in your heart:

I dream . . . ____

____

____.

I dream . . . ____

____

____.

Offer each of these to God. Let him know that if it is time to set aside a dream that is yours and not from him, you are ready to do it. Also, declare to God that if he wants you to keep pursuing a dream, you need his power and you will press on.

DREAMING GOD'S DREAMS

One way to be sure your dreams line up with the heart of God is to adopt his dreams. One of God's biggest longings is for people to come to faith in his beloved Son, Jesus. Read Matthew 9:36–38 and reflect on the heart of Jesus.

Write the names of a few people you love who are not followers of Jesus:

I love . . . ____.

I love . . . ____.

I love . . . ____.

Pray for God to capture your heart with his dream for each of these people to come to faith in Jesus. Ask him, "Holy Spirit, give me your wisdom, boldness, and the right words to share your faith naturally with each of these people."

PRAYER ECHOES

Hannah faced unfair pain, relational attacks, unwarranted accusations from a prophet, unhelpful words from her husband, a sense of abandonment from God, and the realization that dreams do not always come true. Yet, with blurred eyes filled with hot tears and a broken heart, she never stopped praying. What an example to follow! And this is not the end of her story. In the next lesson, we will hear a whole different kind of prayer from this woman of faith.

LESSON 11

HANNAH (PART 2)

Praying When You Just Can't Hold Back Your Joy

1 SAMUEL 1:21–2:11

HER NEED

MEETING HANNAH

Sometimes dreams do come true after a long time of waiting. Sometimes there are moments of incredible victory. Life does have times when joy invades our soul with indescribable power. What do we do when this happens? Is it OK to express how we are really feeling? Should I let celebration erupt from my soul and shout for joy when so many others near me and around the world are struggling? These are fair questions.

The prayer we will experience in this lesson also comes from Hannah's heart and lips. Time has passed. Her prayers lifted up with moans and through tears have been answered in the affirmative, and she has conceived and borne a son. This prayer comes as Hannah and her son, Samuel, come to the house of the Lord at Shiloh, and Hannah encounters the influential prophet Eli again. She reminds Eli of their last encounter (politely leaving out the part where he had wrongly accused her of being drunk). On this occasion, Hannah needs to rejoice and offer praise!

Hannah begins her prayer with these words:

> *"My heart rejoices in the LORD;*
> *in the LORD my horn is lifted high.*
> *My mouth boasts over my enemies,*
> *for I delight in your deliverance.*
>
> *There is no one holy like the LORD;*
> *there is no one besides you;*
> *there is no Rock like our God."*
>
> **—1 Samuel 2:1–2**

READ: 1 SAMUEL 1:21–2:11

REFLECT

> *"He raises the poor from the dust*
> *and lifts the needy from the ash heap;*
> *he seats them with princes*
> *and has them inherit a throne of honor."*
>
> **—1 Samuel 2:8**

HER STORY

Hannah had no words in her time of darkness and pain, only groaning. Now she is a poet and songwriter who can't stop praising God. Can this be the same woman? Of course!

Hannah's story is one of radical change and steady consistency. When we pick up this second part of Hannah's prayer journey, some things have dramatically changed in her life. Before her prayer in 1 Samuel 1, Hannah was barren. Her womb was empty, and her heart was shattered. Tears marked her cheeks, and her prayers were uttered and muttered through clenched teeth. Now in 1 Samuel 2 her heart overflows, and her prayers are shouted from the highest rooftop. Boldness marks Hannah's prayers and joy is alive in her eyes and through her words. In a sense, everything has changed.

Just before her prayer in 1 Samuel 2, we see that Hannah is fundamentally the same woman she was before God answered her. Prayer remained central in her life when times were hard *and* when everything seemed to be coming up roses. She trusted God to be present and powerful when the answer to her biggest prayer was no (or, better yet, wait). She also saw God as sovereign and on the throne of heaven when the answer to her heart's cry was a heavenly yes. Hannah loved her Creator when she was barren, and also when she was breastfeeding.

What an example to women of faith throughout history! Prayer is for the highs and the lows of life. God is faithful when we get what we ask of him and when he wisely says, "No," or "Wait." Hannah's prayer journey through both the valleys of sorrow and heights of celebration stands as a beautiful example for all of us who ride the roller coaster we call life.

MY NEED

Some people hold back their praise, celebration, and joy. They think to themselves: *Who am I to feel so blessed? Why would I experience such goodness? Is this even fair?* When God answers prayer, when dreams come true, when provision is opulent, when community is sweet—these moments call us to prayers of praise. Don't hold back!

- Was there a time something good happened in your life and you held back from celebrating and rejoicing with others because you felt bad that you felt so good? Or maybe your caution was based on a worry that others might not rejoice with you. Ask God to give you the courage to praise his name publicly and not hold back.

- Who do you have in your life that will always be excited when something good and beautiful has happened in your life? Cherish these dear people.

- The apostle Paul says to people in the church (the body of Christ): "If one part suffers, every part suffers with it; if one part is honored, every part rejoices with it" (1 Corinthians 12:26). Do all you can to free others to celebrate their joys out loud and in front of you, knowing that you truly do rejoice with them.

LESSONS FROM HANNAH

1. **Lift up a joyful heart.** At the start of this prayer, Hannah is overflowing with joy and delight. She can hardly contain it. What an example for us! When God shows up and moves, unleash praise and celebration. It pleases him and is good for our soul. Don't hold it in!

2. **Pray with a spirit of victory.** Deliverance! Victory! Now Hannah sees how God has set her free. Not only does she notice how God has won the battle in her life, but she recounts how he has delivered his people in the past and the present. What a reminder to see and acknowledge God's liberating work!

MY REFLECTIONS

What is God teaching me about prayer through this prayer of Hannah?

1. What was a time when you were overflowing with joy and awareness of God's goodness? How did this impact the way you prayed and what you prayed about?

2. What is a victory you have seen God win in your life or the life of a person you are close to? What are ways this reality can move you to lift up prayers of bold celebration?

3. When you think of how God moved in Hannah's life and the ways that he has been active in your life, what are some of the key characteristics of God you see at work? What are some of God's divine attributes that move you to lift up energetic praise?

OUR PRAYER

AN INVITATION TO PRAISE AND CELEBRATION

Write a note, email, text message, or some other form of communication to someone close to you sharing something wonderful God has done in your life. This is not about being prideful but rather about humbly giving God glory. Like Hannah, get public with your prayer of praise. Invite others to celebrate God's goodness.

> Dear (name),
>
> I am reaching out to share something amazing God has done. I know you will rejoice with me and ask that you lift up a prayer of praise with me.
>
> (Add your note about God's work, protection, provision, movement of power . . . anything great he has done here.)
>
> Thank you and may God's richest blessings be on you,
>
> (Your Name) ______________________________

Send this to the people you believe will celebrate with you.

PRAYING LIKE HANNAH

Use the prompts below to write a prayer of praise using themes you learn from Hannah.

Celebrate God's goodness:

- ______________________________
- ______________________________

Declare his deliverance:

- ______________________________
- ______________________________

Describe his attributes:

- ______________________________
- ______________________________

Ask God to humble the proud:

- ______________________________
- ______________________________

Pray for God's sovereign rule:

- ______________________________
- ______________________________

PRAYER ECHOES

Hannah was piercingly honest and cried out to God through tears when times were hard. She also prayed with equal passion and expressiveness when things were going great. Let's seek to do the same.

LESSON 12

ABIGAIL

Praying for Courageous Action

1 SAMUEL 25

HER NEED

MEETING ABIGAIL

Problems in life can come to us fast and furious from inside the home, from our relational life, from uncontrolled outside forces, and from just about anywhere. Often these surprise challenges hit us with no warning, and we need wisdom to work through them. If you want to learn how to navigate and pray through these times of life, take a walk and learn from a wise woman of action named Abigail.

Her name could be translated several ways, and all of them are beautiful. Abigail can mean: "My Father's joy," "My Father is exalted," or "My Father is joyful." She lived in a highly complex time. The great prophet and leader, Samuel, had just died, and it was a season of mourning and uncertainty. Saul was king, but his heart had turned from God. David would soon become king over the people, and Samuel had anointed him for this role. This drove King Saul mad, and he was on the hunt to find David and execute him.

We meet Abigail as she encounters David when he is on the run from Saul. To top it all off, Abigail was married to a very wealthy man who was a cruel fool and a short-tempered drunk. That is a lot of complexity in the life of this godly and wise woman.

READ: 1 SAMUEL 25

REFLECT

David said to Abigail, "Praise be to the Lord, the God of Israel, who has sent you today to meet me."

—1 Samuel 25:32

HER STORY

It was an arranged marriage. Abigail did not choose Nabal, but he was her husband nonetheless. He was foolish, filled with anger, lacking wisdom, and often under the influence of too much strong drink. This was her daily existence with Nabal.

In all of this, Abigail knew God. Though we do not have a record of a specific prayer of Abigail in the pages of Scripture, her courageous actions of faith reveal her heart and boldness. She was a woman of faith. She listened to Yahweh and was quick to respond to his promptings. Because of her husband's sharp tongue and selfish streak, Abigail was given an opportunity to exercise her life of prayer and faith.

Although David and his men had graciously protected and watched over Nabal's business dealings, Nabal foolishly insulted them. In response, the wrath of David, the giant slayer, headed Nabal's way like a tsunami. David's wave of judgment would wash over Nabal and his whole household. Nothing could stop it! Well, almost nothing!

God *did not* send an army to stop David and spare him from a foolish act of knee-jerk vengeance. God *did not* send a master negotiator to talk David off the ledge of his own anger. Instead, the God of heaven sent a woman named Abigail, who did not bring a sword but instead offered gentle wisdom, poetic words, and a delicious lunch to David.

Abigail stopped David and his men in their tracks. One woman who listened to God and dared to take immediate action stopped David from dishonoring God by taking vengeance into his own hands.

When David finally understood what was happening, he saw the story behind the story. Remember, this is the man who stood in front of Goliath and knew that God would deliver him. Now David's mighty army came against one woman, and God won again. Vengeance was averted, and David recognized what was happening. As the cloud of his anger dissipated, he recognized the fingerprints of God on the situation.

> *David said to Abigail, "Praise be to the Lord, the God of Israel, who has sent you today to meet me. May you be blessed for your good judgment and for keeping me from bloodshed this day and from avenging myself with my own hands."*
>
> **—1 Samuel 25:32–33**

Abigail heard from God. Standing in a ravine, she listened to Yahweh, fully aware that she could be trampled. In faith, she believed the word of the Lord and dared to follow at great cost. May we learn from her example and be women whose prayer lives are so tuned in to God's guidance that when we hear, we move as the Spirit leads. No matter what the cost. Without waiting. With trust and humility.

MY NEED

Unexpected and uninvited challenges face us almost every day. If we are honest with ourselves, we don't know how to respond to many of these. Prayer is the answer, as we pray: "God of heaven, give me eyes to see your way forward, grant me courage to act, and fortify me for whatever lies ahead."

- What challenges are you facing, and how much time do you spend crying out to God for wisdom?

- What unexpected confrontation has hit your life, and are you ready to stand up and face it in the power of the Holy Spirit who lives in you?

- Is there a challenge you are avoiding and don't want to tackle? Pause right now and ask God to give you a spirit like Abigail.

LESSONS FROM ABIGAIL

1. **When God is clearly leading, and the situation demands it, be ready to act quickly.** Sometimes we overprocess, drag our feet, and justify delaying action when God is calling us to move. Abigail is praised for acting quickly (1 Samuel 25:18). She had to. If she stalled, David and his army would have stopped only after vengeance was poured out. Pausing, praying more, and gathering wisdom is often the way to go. But in some situations, the response God is leading you toward is immediate prayer-led action.

2. **Your story is still being written.** As you finished reading 1 Samuel 25, you may have noticed that this faithful woman who suffered under Nabal's foolishness and cruelty ended up in the palace married to David. What an example and inspiration for us to rise up when we feel that life's circumstances are holding us down! Never forget that God is still writing your story when times are hard.

3. **Overcoming unimaginable odds is not just when David stands against Goliath.** God loves to show his presence and power through all of his servants. Abigail stood against an army of four hundred mighty soldiers led by a famous giant slayer. And you know how her story ended. Dare to stand against the odds and see what God can do through you.

MY REFLECTIONS

What is God teaching me about prayer through Abigail's listening and quick actions?

1. What is one action of obedience you know God is calling you to take, but you have been holding back? What will it take for you to move into humble action?

2. What is a life circumstance that is holding you down, discouraging you, or keeping you from fully following Jesus' will for your life? How can you rise above this?

3. We all face hard circumstances when it seems there is no way to win, overcome, or press through. What are you facing that seems insurmountable, and how can others help you walk in God's power and victory in this area?

OUR PRAYER

MOVE ME TO ACTION-ORIENTED PRAYER

Sit in silence and ask God if there are actions he wants you to take in your life. Write down at least one thing you believe God wants you to do now—no waiting or stalling! When you have acted, write down the results.

My action: ______________________________

The results: ______________________________

STAND AGAINST THE TSUNAMI

Tsunamis of sin are flooding our world, culture, and families. Evil is real, and the enemy is at work. Write down a few examples of these onslaughts of Satan:

The tsunami of ______________________________.

The tsunami of ______________________________.

The tsunami of ______________________________.

Pray for God's hand to stop each of these and then ask God if there is one that you should take action and stand against. If you sense God's call, step in as he leads.

PRAYER ECHOES

In a time of turmoil and in the midst of a painful marriage, Abigail heard from the Lord. Her ears were still open. Her heart was tender. Her life was surrendered so that she was ready to move into action. No matter what you are facing, God still loves you. He is near. He is speaking. Be ready to respond with humble obedience.

LESSON 13

THE WIDOW OF ZAREPHATH

Praying in Great Need

1 KINGS 17:7–24;
LUKE 4:25–26

HER NEED

MEETING THE WIDOW OF ZAREPHATH

Moments of need hit all of our lives. Often these moments arise in unexpected ways, and they are always unwanted. Yet in these times of famine, drought, and emptiness, God seems to show up in profound and deep ways. These are often the moments we pray with greater passion and see miraculous results.

The widow of Zarephath is not remembered by her name. Instead, she is known for her defining life situation. The great prophet Elijah knew her name, and it would have been precious to him because the Lord used her to provide food and shelter in a time of drought and famine. Because of her willingness to be hospitable, God also saved the widow and her son.

This faithful woman was born and raised in a place where worship of Yahweh was rare and devotion to Baal (the Canaanite god of storm and fertility) was the norm. She lived in Sidon, a town in the region of Phoenicia. As a widow, she had no protection, no provision, and no safety net. When we meet her, she and her son are starving to death.

READ: 1 KINGS 17:7–24; LUKE 4:25–26

REFLECT

"For this is what the LORD, the God of Israel, says: 'The jar of flour will not be used up and the jug of oil will not run dry until the day the LORD sends rain on the land.'" . . . Then the woman said to Elijah, "Now I know that you are a man of God and that the word of the LORD from your mouth is the truth."

—1 Kings 17:14, 24

HER STORY

Almost everyone prays at some time in their life. Even atheists are said to become very religious and prayerful when they are in a foxhole and enemy bullets are whizzing over their heads.

This widow from Zarephath would have been taught to call out to the god Baal in times of need. Even if she was not particularly religious, she would likely pray for rain and crops to grow. It is hard to imagine any mother not praying if she was watching her child starve to death.

Here is the problem: Prayers lifted to an idol or false god fall on deaf ears. Lifeless statues made of stone, wood, and even gold have no power. But something extraordinary happens. This widow of Zarephath is heard by the God of heaven. All through the Bible, we read that our God cares about the forgotten and needy. In particular, God provides for widows and calls his people to do the same.

Before God sent Elijah to the home of this woman, he had already prepared the way. In 1 Kings 17:9, we read God instructing the prophet, "Go at once to Zarephath in the region of Sidon and stay there. I have directed a widow there to supply you with food." The Lord of heaven had spoken to this widow and directed her to provide food for the prophet even before he arrived on her doorstep. Though she and her son were starving and she was planning their final meal, this widow was ready to respond to the word of a God she did not know.

Elijah was a fugitive. A man on the run. Jezebel, the evil queen and wife of King Ahab, wanted the prophet dead. As he was running for his life, Elijah ended up in the same region (Sidon) that Jezebel was from. One woman from Sidon, the queen of Israel, wanted Elijah dead. Another woman, a poor and starving widow from Sidon, was used by God to keep him alive. What a stunning contrast!

This short little story is filled with surprises. When Elijah asks the widow to feed him with the last food she had, he promises that his God, Yahweh, would miraculously keep her flour and oil jars filled and overflowing as long as needed. She does it, and God shows up in daily provision. When her son dies, she asks for Elijah's help. The prophet prays over her son, and her son breathes again. When all of this happens, the widow finally gets it. Elijah's God is the true God!

The widow had spent a lifetime praying to the idolatrous gods of her people. It was all she knew. But here the God of heaven heard her prayer and showed up in her moment of deepest need. What a story of God meeting the needs of a woman whom no one else cared about!

She is a woman whose name we do not know. She was loved by a God whose name she did not know. By the faithful service of God's prophet, this widow learned to pray to the God whose name she learned from Elijah. She finally met the one true Lord of heaven who knew her name before she was born.

MY NEED

Financial resources can run low or even disappear. Relational support can wane, and we end up feeling alone and unsupported. Our body can get weary, sick, and bruised and our energy reserves can become depleted. The widow in this story learned that God is the source of unlimited resources.

- Where are you running low on what you need to make it through the day? Do you believe God is able to provide?

- Who has God placed in your life to be a mentor in faith and trust? The widow had Elijah. Who do you have in your life, and what is God teaching you through this person?

- How has God provided in surprising ways in the past, and why should this give you confidence to trust him for the future?

LESSONS FROM THE WIDOW OF ZAREPHATH

1. **God knows our names and hears our prayers, even before we know his name.** God was caring for this widow before she knew who he was. In his sovereign wisdom and care, God hears every prayer. Take confidence in this God who listens to us!

2. **God loves to meet the daily needs of the needy.** Flour and oil seem so simple and common, but in a drought and famine they are the ingredients needed to make the bread that keeps a person alive. God took delight in giving food to a prophet, a widow, and her son. Don't forget that even simple needs are met by the infinite God of heaven.

3. **God uses miracles to show that he is real, near, and powerful.** The widow experienced a big miracle—her son was brought back to life. But she also experienced a comparatively small miracle—having enough oil and flour for one more day. But both miracles brought life! These miracles were part of what God used to convince a pagan woman who he was—the true God of the storm, fertility, harvest, and everything else. We can trust our God!

MY REFLECTIONS

What is God teaching me about his heart and prayer through the widow of Zarephath?

1. What is one way God cared for you and showed that he knew you before you placed your faith in his name?

2. How have you seen God care for the needy in your community, and how might you and your church join God on his mission of providing for those in need?

3. What great need do you have today? How can you lift this up to God and trust that he cares and is ready to draw near to you in your time of need?

OUR PRAYER

LORD, HELP THE NEEDY AND USE ME

Write a brief and courageous prayer asking God to use you to extend help, care, and kindness to someone who is hurting today.

Lord, please help:

God of miraculous provision, please use me as a conduit of provision and care for someone in my neighborhood, church, or community in the coming days. Help me see the need and take action. Amen.

PRAYING FOR COMMUNITY MINISTRIES

Identify a few ministries that help the poor, hungry, and forgotten in your area.

Ministry name: ______________________________

Needs they meet: ______________________________

Ministry name: ______________________________

Needs they meet: ______________________________

Ministry name: ______________________________

Needs they meet: ______________________________

Take a little time and review their website and pray for them to minister to needy people in your community. If you feel led to partner, find a way you can support one of these ministries by giving or serving.

PRAYER ECHOES

The widow of Zarephath would have spent a lifetime praying to pagan gods, idols, and the sky above. She had no idea that the God of heaven was watching her, looking out for her, and that he knew her name. Though her gods never answered, Yahweh did. He gave bread, life, and hope, and even sent a prophet to her home. Let's never forget that our God loves the outcast, and we are called to love and pray for them too.

LESSON 14

HULDAH

Praying with Trembling and Courage

2 CHRONICLES 34

HER NEED

MEETING HULDAH

Huldah lived and served God in a time when there was a national rebellion against God. After several decades of evil ruling the land through the leadership of King Manasseh and his son King Amon, Josiah became the king at eight years of age.

Josiah began to seek the face and ways of Yahweh. At twenty years old, with the full authority of the kingship, Josiah began to cleanse the land of sin and the people of their rebellion. He repaired the temple of God because it was in absolute shambles. In this process, the people found the book of the law. When Josiah read the words of God, he realized that the nation was living in radical rebellion to the ways of Yahweh. This young and passionate king needed wisdom and insight on what to do next.

This is where Huldah comes in. Rather than go to Jeremiah or Zephaniah (who were both prophets at that time), Josiah called on the prophetess Huldah for wisdom, insight, and connection with God. She was deeply trusted and seen as a source of godly wisdom. In a time of spiritual renewal, she was called on for her insight by the king of the nation. When she spoke for the Lord, she dared to say exactly what God placed on her heart, even if it would be hard for some people to hear. Huldah was a prophetess who sought the Lord's wisdom on behalf of his people. She was a servant of Yahweh who was used to bring reform and revival to the land.

READ: 2 CHRONICLES 34

REFLECT

Tell the king of Judah, who sent you to inquire of the LORD, "This is what the LORD, the God of Israel, says concerning the words you heard: Because your heart was responsive and you humbled yourself before God when you heard what he spoke against this place and its people, and because you humbled yourself before me and tore your robes and wept in my presence, I have heard you, declares the LORD. Now I will gather you to your ancestors, and you will be buried in peace. Your eyes will not see all the disaster I am going to bring on this place and on those who live here."

–2 Chronicles 34:26–28

HER STORY

Not everyone liked what God had to say through his prophets. Huldah was committed to speak the word of the Lord even when the message might bring conviction or land on a resistant heart. She knew about the risks connected to her calling and ministry.

We do not have a record of a specific prayer lifted up to heaven by Huldah. Yet we do know that she sought the Lord on behalf of Josiah and received a message to send back to the king. As a prophetess and woman of God living in a time of moral compromise and religious apostasy, Huldah could have been moved to pray some very passionate prayers:

- God of heaven, remove, dethrone, or change the heart of any king standing against the will of Yahweh.

- Holy Ruler of heaven, bring repentance and hope to our wayward nation.

- Thank you for raising up a new king (Josiah). Protect this young boy from the political forces that would want to remove or assassinate him. Keep his eyes fixed on you and not on the powers of this world.

Huldah was on the inside of the political and religious community but not tainted by the river of compromise and rebellion that had been flowing through her nation. She sat in the city center and was accessible to the people. She was there as a conduit of God's words.

When the young, passionate, and godly King Josiah sent ambassadors to her, she did what they asked. She inquired of the Lord. Then, the God of heaven answered. We can imagine Huldah knew that sometimes the answer to her prayers came with a soft and gentle tone and she could pass it along with confidence that the hearer would be thankful. At other times, the answer from heaven came crashing down with the weight of heavenly judgment. This word from the Lord was the latter.

What happened next was nothing short of miraculous! Josiah renewed the covenant with God. After decades of compromise and national sin, the people pledged to follow the ways of God and the teaching of his law. And then the people cleaned house! Out with the idols, down with false worship, and away with deceptive leaders. Huldah was the messenger of God and a prophetess involved in this revival.

MY NEED

Have you ever had to confront a friend with bad news? Remember the time you needed to speak a hard truth to a family member? Have you ever felt the knot in your gut when you were certain that the Holy Spirit wanted you to correct someone with kindness, but you knew they would not take it well? Welcome to the world of Huldah! If you want to learn to prayerfully navigate these pathways, walk with her and learn from her example.

- When was a time someone came to you and brought a correction or rebuke? Did you receive it humbly or push back?

- Who is a person in your life who needs a loving and firm word of correction? Is God calling you to speak with kindness, love, and firm truth?

- Why is it essential that we bathe these moments in prayer not only before they occur or during those moments but also after they happen?

LESSONS FROM HULDAH

1. **God speaks when his servants are ready to listen.** Huldah was a prophetess, so she uniquely heard from the Lord. As God's people today, we can still hear from our Maker. Jesus said how his sheep listen to his voice (John 10:3). Remember that Jesus Christ—who is the same yesterday, today, and forever—still speaks to us today (Hebrews 13:8).

2. **Scripture moves us to prayer**. When the workers find the law of God buried in the rubble of the temple area, they read it to King Josiah, and he is moved to repentance, confession, and prayer. When you read the Scriptures, let them move you to seek the face of God.

3. **Sometimes answers to prayer are not what we might expect or want, but they are always good**. When Josiah got the answer to his inquiry from God (through Huldah), it was hard news. But it led to national repentance and a great season of obedience to God. When you get an answer to prayer that is not exactly what you want, trust the God who rules over heaven and earth.

MY REFLECTIONS

What is God teaching me about prayer through Huldah?

1. What are Scriptures that move you to pray, be it a prayer of praise, confession, thanksgiving, or supplication?

2. Huldah and Josiah inspired each other in both faith and prayer. Who is a person that you can begin praying with more often, and what is one step you can take to pray more in partnership with others?

3. What is one hard answer to prayer that you have received? How did you eventually discover that God was showing his wisdom and mercy in this hard answer?

OUR PRAYER

Lord, teach me to rebuke with honest humility, if this is your will.

Read 2 Chronicles 34:23–28 a few times. Get the heartbeat of this rebuke and honest declaration Huldah sent to Josiah. Also, notice God's grace in the truth being declared.

Write a humble but bold prayer asking God to use you to speak truth in love to those who need it.

A TREMBLING PRAYER

Ask yourself, "What is something that I tremble to pray about?" Maybe you don't want to know the answer.

As you learn from Huldah, refuse to avoid the hard prayers. Ask God to show you a person in your life who needs someone to come and speak a hard and loving truth about their drinking, attitude, harsh words, waning faith, whatever it is. As you pray, be ready to respond if the Holy Spirit leads you to have a conversation with this person.

PRAYER ECHOES

Learn from Huldah's example of courageous prayer and how she spoke even when it was dangerous. Pray with increasing confidence and courage, believing God can use you even when you feel unworthy and afraid.

LESSON 15

ESTHER

Praying When Your Burden Is Too Great

ESTHER 4:6–16

HER NEED

MEETING ESTHER

The situation was intense. The burden was great. Esther needed other people to join her and support her because she could not bear what she was facing alone. What an example of wisdom! When she realized that she needed others to support her, she cried out for help.

Esther lived in a perilous time when standing up for her faith could be costly, but she was willing to count the cost. What an example for us! We can seek the face of God and follow him in the dangerous times we face. Like Esther, we can find community in this challenging journey.

Esther's people had been exiled by the Babylonians and forced to assimilate into the ways of their captors. Then the Babylonian Empire was conquered by the Persians, the current rulers of her land. This would have made her feel displaced both physically and spiritually. To make things even more complex, she had been chosen by King Xerxes to be his new queen. In a jealous rage, one of the king's closest confidants was doing all he could to have the Jews in the land annihilated. It is in this perilous setting that we see Esther's faith come alive. It would have been easy for Esther to remain silent. She could have blended in, refused to stand out, and stayed isolated. Instead, with bold courage she stood, spoke, asked others to partner with her, and risked everything for the sake of her people.

READ: ESTHER 4:6–16

REFLECT

Go, gather together all the Jews who are in Susa, and fast for me. Do not eat or drink for three days, night or day. I and my attendants will fast as you do. When this is done, I will go to the king, even though it is against the law. And if I perish, I perish.

—Esther 4:16

HER STORY

One very interesting insight about the book of Esther is that the name of God is never mentioned. It is the only book in the entire Bible where this is the case. What is truly ironic is that the fingerprints of God and his sovereign leading are all over this book, even though his name is never explicitly mentioned.

Esther's story is embedded in the exile of God's people after the invasion and destruction of Jerusalem by the king of Babylon. The Jewish people had been living in Babylon for several decades before the Persians took over. The new Persian rulers allowed some of the Jewish exiles to return to Jerusalem to repopulate the destroyed holy city. However, other Jews chose to continue living in Persia. Esther was part of the remnant that remained in Persia. We don't know the full details, but the Bible says that Esther was an orphan and had suffered the loss of both her parents.

Through a series of dramatic events, the previous queen of Persia lost her throne, and King Xerxes held a national beauty contest to find a new queen. Through God's sovereign guidance behind the scenes (a big theme in the book of Esther) and Esther's gracious wisdom, she won the contest and stepped onto the throne.

Following Esther's rise to the throne, in a series of complex and tense interactions, Esther's trusted caretaker and cousin Mordecai and Haman, a leader in Xerxes's government, come into conflict with one another. The book of Esther reveals that due to Mordecai's refusal to bow to him, Haman wanted all the Jewish people destroyed and their possessions stolen. He plotted and planned their demise, and he thought he had it all figured out. What he did not know was that Esther's God was watching out for his people, and Esther was a wise and fearless adversary who was ready to risk her own life to deliver her people.

Esther called her people from all over the capital city of Susa to fast and pray for her before she appeared before the king to protect her people. Esther requested these prayers because, according to Persian law, anyone who entered the king's throne room uninvited could be executed. Esther needed the fortification that comes from community. What happened next was an epic turning of the tables worthy of a full-length movie! The king welcomed Esther into his presence, and through her exalted actions God's people were delivered from Haman's plot. Moreover, Mordecai would be vindicated of

Haman's attacks , and justice would be poured out on Haman, the enemy of the Jewish people.

In remembrance of Esther's bravery, a festival was created in her honor. The Feast of Purim is still celebrated to this day to remember how God saved his people from what looked like certain destruction. The prayers of Esther and the people made such an impact that the repercussion is still felt in the world today.

MY NEED

Our world is a dangerous place. If we are going to follow Jesus, we will need courage far beyond our own. We need heavenly boldness. We must have the strength of community. We might not be risking our lives by coming to a king uninvited, but standing up for Jesus and living with uncompromising faith comes with potentially costly consequences. If we are going to learn from Esther and walk with this bold sister, we need to begin by praying, "Lord, I will follow you, no matter what the cost," and be ready to invite others to pray for you.

- What consequences have you faced when you committed to follow Jesus in a situation where others did not? Reflect on how God showed up and carried you through those times.

- What is a situation you are facing where it would be easier to be a silent and hidden Christian? Invite God to show you ways to stand up for your faith, and invite other Christians to pray for you and stand with you.

LESSONS FROM ESTHER

1. **Prayer in peril.** When times are hard, when persecution arises, when tension is thick—PRAY! Never be hesitant to come to God in the hard times; his arms are wide open. Yes, it is good to pray when the seas are calm and everything seems to be coming up roses. But never miss a chance to pray when you are in the middle of the storm and the skies are dark for as far as your eyes can see.

2. **Prayer in community.** Esther could have prayed on her own, but she knew better. The call to fast was clearly linked to a call to prayer. Even though she was in a pagan land, Esther knew that power came through praying to the one true God. When you are in perilous times, get as many people as you can to pray and fast. Then, watch God show up in power!

3. **Prayer and fasting.** Throughout Scripture, there has always been a connection between prayer and fasting. There are times when we really need to focus on prayer and be moved to deeper places of crying out to God. Fasting helps. It gets our attention and removes all the distractions of food. As we hunger for physical sustenance, we can be moved to pray more. Seek out how you can integrate the practice of fasting into your prayer life.

MY REFLECTIONS

What is God teaching me about prayer through Esther?

1. What was a situation when you faced peril and danger? How did you pray and what difference did that prayer make in your heart and the situation?

2. When you face a hard time in your life (or walk with a loved one through such a time), who are the people that you would most naturally invite to join you in prayer (and fasting)? What are you facing right now that might move you to ask this circle of prayer partners to support you and join you in prayer?

OUR PRAYER

FINGERPRINT PRAYERS

Read the book of Esther in one sitting. Write down the times that God is present and working in his sovereign power (even when he is not mentioned by name):

When God was at work: ______

What God did: ______

When God was at work: ______

What God did: ______

When God was at work: ______

What God did: ______

When God was at work: ______

What God did: ______

When God was at work: ______________________________

What God did: ______________________________

When God was at work: ______________________________

What God did: ______________________________

When God was at work: ______________________________

What God did: ______________________________

Look at each way God worked in Esther's story and thank him for the ways he shows up in your life (sometimes unnoticed).

PRAYER TEAM

We all need prayer support. Consider asking a couple of people to pray for you regularly (at least once a week). Give them help by sending a monthly text with two or three current prayer items. You might even want to gather with them in person or on a video chat once a month for prayer.

Names of people to invite to be on my prayer team:

- ______________________________
- ______________________________
- ______________________________
- ______________________________
- ______________________________

PRAYER ECHOES

Esther called on a large group of people to support her in fasting and prayer. If you don't have a team of people around you in regular prayer for your life and those you love, seriously consider identifying a person or two you trust who will pray for you and reach out to them with a present need.

LESSON 16

THE SHUNAMMITE WOMAN

Asking for Intercession

2 KINGS 4:8–37

HER NEED

MEETING THE SHUNAMMITE WOMAN

Though she is unnamed, the Shunammite woman is one of the most memorable women in the Bible. She also has holy perception that Elisha is a man of God, and when she needs intercession, she knows where to go for help.

The Shunammite woman is not a poor peasant without access to resources and would have been considered wealthy, but her need is beyond physical provision. Her beloved child falls ill and dies in her arms. Her path is one of joy followed by woe—a path many women have walked in all kinds of scenarios. When this happens, she goes to Elisha for help, falls at his feet, and fervently asks for prayer.

READ: 2 KINGS 4:8–37

REFLECT

So she set out and came to the man of God at Mount Carmel.

When he saw her in the distance, the man of God said to his servant Gehazi, "Look! There's the Shunammite! Run to meet her and ask her, 'Are you all right? Is your husband all right? Is your child all right?'"

"Everything is all right," she said.

—2 Kings 4:25–26

HER STORY

The Shunammite woman is not afraid to take initiative. When we first meet her, we see that she is observant of Elisha's coming and going through Shunem. She observes not only his coming and going but also that he is "a holy man of God" (2 Kings 4:9). She then shows him hospitality, inviting him in for dinner. Then, she takes further initiative and suggests to her husband that they build a small room for him on their roof, a little guest house with a bed, a chair, a table, and a lamp, where he can stay when he passes through. She has thought of everything.

In response to her hospitality, Elisha offers whatever help she needs. During the conversation that ensues, Elisha's servant, Gehazi, makes it clear that she has no child. Elisha then says that she will hold a son in her arms in about a year's time. Elisha tells her this will happen, but her heart is so tender at first that she begs him not to mislead her. This is a prayer she has not uttered herself and may even be willing to say out loud. She doesn't want false hope and seems wary of miracles and promises at this point in the story.

Elisha's prophecy does come to pass, and she gives birth to a son. The child grows until he is old enough to work in the field with his father and the reapers, but he suddenly becomes sick and is taken to his mother, who holds him while he tragically dies in her arms. It's a scene of great sadness.

As soon as this happens, the Shunammite woman sets out to find Elisha for help. She places her son on Elisha's bed in the guest room, and then she goes to find him. She doesn't simply send for Elisha. She gets on a donkey herself and goes to Mount Carmel to find him. Even when Gehazi, a messenger, asks her to communicate what she needs to him, she doesn't turn back from where she is going. She is determined to reach the holy man of God herself and ask him to intercede for her. When she finds him, she falls at his feet and reminds him that she specifically asked not to have her hopes raised only to have them disappointed.

Elisha offers to send Gehazi back to the boy with his staff, but the Shunammite woman insists Elisha go with her. Elisha then decides to return with her, and in one of the few stories of someone being raised from the dead in the Bible, her boy is brought back to life. Elisha goes into the room with the boy, prays, and then the boy's cold body becomes warm again. The story ends with this compassionate, competent, self-reliant, maternal woman reunited with her son.

MY NEED

What will I do when tragedy strikes and I need help? Is there any prayerful person who may come to help me? To intercede on my behalf? When I am afraid to hope, is there anyone who can help me find hope again? Do I ask for help in prayer when I need it?

- Do you know who you can go to when you need help? Are you perceptive of how God is working in the lives of others to such an extent that you will know where to go for help when you need it?

- When you feel a need but are afraid to utter it for fear of disappointment, how can you trust in the Lord our God to listen, respond, and show you mercy and compassion? In what ways can you change your heart to trust him with your every need?

- Are you establishing a foundation of healthy spiritual and faithful community by showing hospitality and perceiving God's people around you? Will you have a holy community when your time of need arrives?

LESSONS FROM THE SHUNAMMITE WOMAN

1. **Notice holy people.** The Shunammite woman was on the lookout for God's people. In Galatians 5, we learn that the fruits of the Spirit are love, joy, peace, patience, kindness, goodness, faithfulness, gentleness, and self-control. Ask God to help you perceive these fruits in the lives of others. And prepare to be surprised! These fruits are often found in unexpected people.

2. **Take initiative.** Remember that God sometimes calls us to literally go the extra mile like the Shunammite woman did when she pursued Elisha. Ask God to help you know when you're called to such action as you pursue the intercession of others in prayer.

My Reflections

What is God teaching you about prayer through the Shunammite woman?

1. What are some characteristics you saw in the Shunammite woman that God could bring into your prayer life? What does it look like to approach others for help with her courage, insistence, and wisdom?
2. The Shunammite woman was relationally wise. She sought and nurtured spiritual support. Where are you seeking and nurturing spiritual support among people who can pray with you and for you?
3. What are some areas where you are competent? And how are those areas of competence related to your prayer life? For example, the Shunammite woman was competent in the area of discernment.

OUR PRAYER

HELP ME PRAY

In the space below, write a letter to someone asking them to pray for you. Lay out your need, and request their help in praying for you. As the Lord leads, send via text, email, or letter.

PRAYER ECHOES

In 2 Kings 4:30, the Shunammite woman insists to Elisha, "As surely as the Lord lives and as you live, I will not leave you." This is how she convinces Elisha to go to her son. Let's make sure that when we pray and ask others to pray for us, we remember it is the Lord we all bow down to.

LESSON 17

GOMER

Praying When Facing My Sin

HOSEA 1:2–11; 3:1–5

HER NEED

MEETING GOMER

She needed to know if God's forgiveness was big enough to cover her rebellion. She may have wondered if there was any way of coming home after diving back into her past patterns of sin. Gomer's life, family, and marriage became a living illustration of Israel's relationship with God, and it was not a pretty picture.

What do you pray when your soul, heart, and body have been ravaged by sin and immersed in immorality? What do you say to God when you don't even know if you want to repent? How do you cry out to God when you are still steeped in iniquity and blinded by the pain of your own poor moral choices? Gomer learned that grace was still available for the people of God—his arms were open to his wayward children. In a similar way, her husband, Hosea, was ready to find her and bring her home, even before she was ready to release her pain and surrender her rebel heart. Gomer needed God to make her heart tender. She needed to know she was still lovable. She was not sure there was enough grace in heaven or her husband's heart to forgive her. Gomer needed to learn that God is in the forgiveness business, and the vehicle he used to teach her this lesson was a prophet named Hosea.

READ: HOSEA 1:2–11; 3:1–5

REFLECT

When the LORD began to speak through Hosea, the LORD said to him, "Go, marry a promiscuous woman and have children with her, for like an adulterous wife this land is guilty of unfaithfulness to the LORD."

—Hosea 1:2

HER STORY

Hosea the prophet and his wife, Gomer, lived in a time when the people of God were in rebellion and bowing down to false idols and pagan deities. God wanted to paint a picture of hope and grace for the most rebellious of people. Gomer is in the center of the painting. We don't actually hear her pray. We are not even sure if her hard heart became soft. What we can learn from her story is that God calls broken sinners home, even when they feel very far away. This is good news.

Gomer's story plays out like an intricate and dramatic movie. Romance, family, infidelity, abandonment, resistance, restoration, and grace. It is the Old Testament version of the prodigal son story. But rather than a son abandoning his father, it is a wife being unfaithful to her husband. Gomer does not just run away with a man; she offers her body to any man in town who will pay the price. The prophet's wife is for sale in the local brothel.

In her darkest time of running from her husband and God, Gomer discovered that she was still loved. Just like the people of Israel, she was wooed and welcomed, if she was ready to return. The arms and heart of Hosea were open to Gomer. The grace of God was more than enough to cover her greatest mistakes and deepest sin.

In a very real sense, Gomer's story is a powerful portrayal of the gospel. Rebels are brought home. Sinners are loved. Iniquity is not ignored or swept under the rug, but it is dealt with by the God, who can cleanse us and make us new. If you ever feel you have run too far away to come home, learn from Gomer's story. If you think your sin is too great for God's grace to conquer, take a walk with Gomer and learn that God is in the business of welcoming home people with rebellious hearts and fickle faith.

MY NEED

Maybe you feel like the people of Israel. God found you and pledged himself to you in love and faithfulness. But now, like Gomer, you're living a life of rebellion. Your sin might be public and out there for everyone to see. Or, it might be hidden, and only you and God know it is there. In either case, you wonder if you are welcome home to God's grace. You might even doubt that God will hear your prayers or accept your repentance. Maybe you've been here before. You have confessed this same sin ten times, fifty times, it feels like a hundred times. Now you've slipped back into the ruts of the same old sinful patterns.

How can you return? How do you pray? Can you dare to bring the same plea for forgiveness to God that you have brought before?

- Are you ready to humbly come to God and confess, even if it is for the hundredth time for the same sin? His heart and ears are open. Come with humility and come now.

- Are you willing to confess and repent? This means you are ready to turn from whatever the sin is that has captured your heart. Tell God you are sorry and then seek his power to turn and run from that pattern of rebellion.

- Here is the tough part. Are you ready to fully accept God's love? If you humbly confess and repent, you are forgiven. Read 1 John 1:9 as many times as you need to:

If we confess our sins,
he is faithful and just
and will forgive us our sins
and purify us from all unrighteousness.

LESSONS FROM GOMER

1. **God knows our sinful patterns.** Hosea knew Gomer's sins. God knew Israel's rebellion. Similarly, the Lord of heaven who is omniscient and all-knowing knows everything about you, and because God approaches your sins with love, Jesus came to die on the cross for you. Since God knows, confess quickly. Don't fear, and don't delay.

2. **God's arms are open.** Hosea welcomed Gomer home. God rejoices when his people return to him. Jesus spread his arms wide to take the nails and die in our place. Don't run away. Run home and see the Father running to welcome you with open arms.

3. **There is hope for a new beginning.** You don't have to keep slipping back into the same old patterns of sin. God's power is sufficient to free you from the clutches of the enemy and power of sin. Never forget: "No temptation has overtaken you except what is common to mankind. And God is faithful; he will not let you be tempted beyond what you can bear. But when you are tempted, he will also provide a way out so that you can endure it" (1 Corinthians 10:13). Dare to pray for the Holy Spirit to give you power to walk in the path of obedience.

MY REFLECTIONS

What is God teaching me about prayer through Gomer's journey?

1. What is an unfaithful (adulterous) area in my life where I am dishonoring God and living in ongoing sin? Am I ready to give this to my Savior?

2. How has God set me free and reminded me of his cleansing grace in the past? Do I believe he can do it again today?

3. Will I let God lavish me with his love, grace, and forgiveness through the finished work of Jesus on the cross? Am I ready to walk and live in the truth of the gospel?

OUR PRAYER

CALLING SIN WHAT IT IS

We all know the feeling that goes through our hearts when we are trying to justify what we are doing even when we know it is an offense to God. We know the uneasiness in our soul and the knot in our gut. Use some of these prompts and ask the Holy Spirit to speak if you are wandering accidentally (or running intentionally) into sin:

- communicating with someone I should not and crossing lines that are inappropriate (through emails, DMs, texts, letters, phone calls, meetings, etc.)
- gossiping about others
- overeating
- overspending
- worrying
- lying
- misuse of time
- unforgiveness
- an emotional affair
- a physical affair
- some other area of ongoing sin

If one of these strikes your heart, bring it to the Lord in prayer, share it with a trusted friend for prayer and accountability, and seek God's power to repent and change.

PRAYER ECHOES

Gomer discovered that even when her heart was hard and her life was in ruins, she was still pursued and loved. Israel learned the same thing. Open your heart to the piercing and glorious truth that God still loves you, wherever you are and whatever you have done. Call out to him in faith and run home.

LESSON 18

ELIZABETH

Worship as Prayer

LUKE 1:5–25, 39–45

HER NEED

MEETING ELIZABETH

It is hard to worship with joy and passion when you feel oppressed and threatened. But God invites his people to worship in all of life's situations. The truth is, if we only pray and lift up God when everything is going our way, we won't pray very much.

Along with the people of God, Elizabeth would have been praying for the Messiah to come and deliver their nation from the oppression of the Roman government who occupied their homeland. Her people were expecting a political and military leader to arrive and fulfill the ancient prophecies. In the middle of this time of longing, Elizabeth and her husband, Zechariah, were serving Yahweh diligently and keeping their ears and eyes open for any sign of the coming Savior.

Here are some of the things the Scriptures reveal about this fascinating woman:

- Both she and her husband had priestly blood coursing through their veins.
- Both Elizabeth and Zechariah were very old.
- She was barren and could not bear children (up to this point).
- She was righteous in God's sight.
- Elizabeth followed the commands of God with a passionate heart.

The Hebrew name Elizabeth had two distinct translations: "God is my oath" and "a worshiper of God." As a woman of deep faith and abiding faithfulness, both of these fit her beautifully.

READ: LUKE 1:5–25, 39–45

REFLECT

When Elizabeth heard Mary's greeting, the baby leaped in her womb, and Elizabeth was filled with the Holy Spirit. In a loud voice she exclaimed: "Blessed are you among women, and blessed is the child you will bear! But why am I so favored, that the mother of my Lord should come to me?"

—Luke 1:41–43

HER STORY

Elizabeth had become an expert in waiting. In her culture and day, having children was a sign of God's blessing and presence. Elizabeth had so much, but she was still missing something. She longed to be a mother, to bear children, and to experience this unique blessing of God.

Late in life, the waiting had transitioned painfully to resignation that she would never be a mother. Old women don't get pregnant and bear children. She had waited a lifetime, and now she had let the dream fade away. She devoted herself to serving God and growing in righteousness in partnership with her husband.

One day, everything changed. A heavenly messenger appeared to her husband, Zechariah, while he was serving in the temple and brought the most unexpected news possible. His prayers, finally, were answered. His wife would bear a unique child who would prepare the way for the Messiah to enter the world. In the spirit of Elijah, their son (John the Baptist) would help usher in the ministry of the long-awaited Messiah.

Both Elizabeth and Zechariah were surprised by God's gift, but they surrendered to the Lord's leading. Sometime later, her relative Mary (who was now pregnant with Jesus, the Messiah) came to visit Elizabeth's home in the hill country of Judea. During this encounter, Elizabeth became the first woman recorded in the Bible to do two distinct and powerful things. First, she prayed a blessing over the Lord Jesus: "Blessed is the child you will bear!" (Luke 1:42). Next, she was the first to declare the Lordship of Jesus the Messiah: "Why am I so favored, that the mother of my Lord should come to me?" (Luke 1:43).

From barren to fertile. From longing for the coming Messiah to meeting him while still in the womb. From praying for the coming Savior to declaring a blessing over Jesus the Christ while he was still in Mary's womb. What a story of faith!

MY NEED

We need to walk faithfully with God even when the road is long and dusty and there are few places to get a drink along the way. Like Elizabeth, we can worship, pray, and serve Jesus for the long haul, if we purpose in our hearts to worship in every season of life.

- When was a time of profound loss or pain that you still worshiped and did your best to follow Jesus? How did your diligent worship grow your faith?

- Reflect on a time when God showed up, answered prayer, and revealed his power. How did this impact your life as a worshiper?

- What are ways you can keep lifting up praise to God and growing as a worshiper even when the road is hard and life is filled with challenges? Why is this so important?

LESSONS FROM ELIZABETH

1. **Never give up!** Both Elizabeth and Zechariah were in that place where they believed God could do all things, but they were not expecting to have a child in their old age. They had prayed for a child a lot while they were younger. Yet God answered this prayer many, many years later. God's timing is not our timing, but learn this lesson from Elizabeth: Never give up on God's ability and willingness to answer prayer.

2. **Follow God's ways and walk in righteousness.** Before either Mary or Elizabeth became pregnant (each in a miraculous way and at a surprising time), Elizabeth was said to be a keeper of the law and righteous in God's sight. Following God's ways prepares us for the miracles (large and small) that he wants to do in our lives.

3. **Speak words of blessing as often as you can.** Elizabeth extends a blessing three times in this first chapter of Luke. She was quick to speak God's blessings over Mary and Jesus. Learn from this example and speak words of blessing as a normal part of your days.

MY REFLECTIONS

What is God teaching me about prayer through Elizabeth?

1. Is there something you have prayed for a lot in the past but have given up on it or stopped praying about it? How might God want to reignite your prayers for this specific need, dream, or movement of God?

2. Who are people in your life who need a word of blessing and spiritual encouragement? What can you do to speak God's goodness and hope into the life of one of these people?

3. Humility marked the life of Elizabeth. She gently and patiently waited for the Lord's leading in her life. What will it look like for you to humbly follow Jesus in the specific areas of challenge you are facing in the coming months?

OUR PRAYER

MAY THE LORD BLESS YOU

Think of a few people you love and care about and pray this blessing over their lives:

"The Lord bless you
and keep you;
the Lord make his face shine on you
and be gracious to you;
the Lord turn his face toward you
and give you peace."

—**Numbers 6:24–26**

You can personalize this prayer of blessing by replacing "you" with the person's name.

A "LONG, DUSTY, WINDING ROAD" PRAYER

Write down one or two very long and challenging roads you have been walking.

The road of ______________________________.

The road of ______________________________.

Write your own prayer asking for God to sustain you along the way and give you a heart filled with worship even along these specific roads.

PRAYER ECHOES

Elizabeth responded to the Holy Spirit and blessed both Mary and her son, Jesus. Tune your heart and mind to the still, small voice of the Spirit and be ready to respond in prayerful surrender whenever God leads you to bless, declare his truth, or lift up the name of Jesus.

LESSON 19

MARY, MOTHER OF JESUS

Praying as Heaven Listens

LUKE 1:26–56

HER NEED

MEETING MARY, MOTHER OF JESUS

Mary, like every honest person, wondered if heaven could hear her prayers. Like all of us, she likely wondered to herself: *When I pray, does anyone hear? Is heaven open, and is my Maker attentive to my prayers? Do my cries and praises make a difference?* Mary prayed to God and lifted up her praise even when the people around scowled and judged her. Heaven heard and understood; the world did not.

We can imagine Mary was filled with praise and rejoicing but also experienced great sorrow and struggle. Mary would have carried the weight of public questioning and shaming once people knew she was pregnant despite being unmarried. Who would believe that the child growing in her womb was a heavenly gift and not an earthly slip-up?

More than the location of this prayer or Mary's emotional state is its spiritual setting. Angelic messages. Heavenly visitation and divine conception. A willing heart of full surrender as Mary uttered the amazing words, "I am the Lord's servant" (Luke 1:38). She needed to know that heaven was listening, and so do we.

READ: LUKE 1:26–56

REFLECT

And Mary said: "My soul glorifies the Lord and my spirit rejoices in God my Savior, for he has been mindful of the humble state of his servant. From now on all generations will call me blessed, for the Mighty One has done great things for me—holy is his name."

—Luke 1:46-49

HER STORY

When Mary's prayer was lifted up to heaven, there were only two people present: Mary and her relative Elizabeth. Each was pregnant. Neither experienced life the way they had imagined it. For Elizabeth, many decades had passed and so had her dreams of carrying a child in her womb or arms. Mary's experience was dramatically different. She was very young and had not been with a man. What cosmic humor would bring together a young, pregnant virgin girl and an elderly pregnant woman? Both submitted to the Lord's will (with some angelic help). Both rejoiced in God's unique work in their lives.

All of heaven must have watched as Jesus and John the Baptist met for the first time in their mothers' wombs. There was some kind of spiritual connection because Elizabeth was flooded with the presence of the Spirit of God. Her unborn baby leapt inside of Elizabeth in response to this encounter (Luke 1:41).

All of the heavenly hosts must have listened in wonder as Mary declared a prayer that has been read, sung, memorized, and adored for over two thousand years. Her prayer proclaims glory to God, joy in the Savior, awareness of God's care and heavenly provision, and generational mercy. It praises the miracles of the past and those yet to come, expresses confidence in God's rule over the nations and rulers of humanity, and lauds God's provision for the needy and discipline of the proud.

This Holy Spirit–inspired prayer revealed the heart of a young woman with theological insight beyond that of the great rabbis of her day. Mary's words were heard by Elizabeth and in muted tones by Jesus and John in their mothers' wombs. Her prayer was inspired by the Spirit and brought joy to the Father's heart. What a Trinitarian moment!

The last time we read about Mary in the New Testament, she is also in prayer. According to Acts 1, following Jesus' resurrection and ascension into heaven to sit at the right hand of the Father, Mary took part in another birth—the birth of the church. Along with the other disciples, Mary gathered with the community of Jesus followers in constant prayer awaiting the arrival of the Holy Spirit. Pentecost was on the horizon, and the church was about to burst into the world.

Through all of her joy and bitterness, Mary learned that heaven is listening. Prayer matters! When God is giving birth to something new—a baby child or a newborn church—prayer makes a difference. If you want to boost your confidence that heaven hears your prayers and that seeking God makes a difference, take a walk with this powerful woman of faith and learn from her journey.

MY NEED

We will all be misunderstood as we walk through life. This is when we need to pray the most. Will God hear? Yes! Is heaven listening? Absolutely! Should I lift prayers of praise even when there is bitterness in the world? Maybe this is when praise is needed the most.

- Who is a person in your life that does not understand your relationship with Jesus? Keep praying for this person. Don't give up! God is listening.

- Is there someone who actually taunts and makes fun of your faith (overtly or subtly)? Commit to praying for God's hand and grace in their life. God loves to answer these prayers and perform miracles.

LESSONS FROM MARY

1. **Pray with humility.** It is humbling to be a mother even in the best of circumstances. Mary models a whole new level of submission and faithful following as she surrenders to God's surprising plan for her life. May every Christian woman read her prayer and seek to learn from her example.

2. **Glorify God in prayer.** Notice the first words out of Mary's mouth as she declares this magnificent prayer. From the depths of her soul, she gives glory to God. Not a bad way to begin our prayers. Try to follow Mary's example and seek to glorify God in your daily prayers.

3. **Rejoice in your spirit.** When you walk with Jesus, live in his ways, follow his path, and surrender to his Word, your spirit will rejoice in God your Savior. There seems to be a direct connection between our joy level and our alignment with God's directing hand. Mary stayed in step with the Spirit's leading and found herself bursting with joy. Seek out joy in your prayer life as well.

MY REFLECTIONS

What is God teaching me about prayer through Mary?

1. If we pray without confidence that God hears, cares, and answers, how will this impact the way we pray? What are the reasons we should pray with bold confidence even while others mock and don't get it?

2. What are specific kinds of prayer and declarations in prayer that can give glory to God? How can you lean more into prayers that lift up God and glorify his name?

3. God does not treat us according to our sins. He extends mercy again and again. How has God been merciful to you, and how can you respond with deep and heartfelt appreciation for his undeniable mercy?

OUR PRAYER

PRAYING FOR THE RESISTORS

Think of two or three people in your life who don't understand your devotion to Jesus and who push back on your faith. Pray they will come to see, love, and follow the Savior they don't yet believe exists.

PRAYER THEMES OF PRAISE

Write a prayer based on some of the themes from Mary's praise:

- Give glory to God.
- Express joy in your Savior.
- Acknowledge God's care and provision.
- Recognize his mercy through the generations.
- Thank him for miracles.
- Pray for God's rule over the nations.
- Thank him for his provision for the needy and discipline of the proud.

My Prayer:

PRAYER ECHOES

Mary lifts up one of the most robust and theologically rich prayers in the Bible. Seek to take your prayers to deeper places of passion. Meditate on Mary's prayer and let it inspire you to pray with greater theological depth and insight.

LESSON 20

ANNA

Unleashing Praise After a Season of Waiting

LUKE 2:36–38

HER NEED

MEETING ANNA

Anna had been without a husband for several decades. Her home, to a large degree, was the temple. She did not actually live there, but almost every waking hour, Anna was in the temple courtyards worshiping and praying. She longed for the coming Messiah and was in a constant waiting posture.

Anna knew pain. She knew loss. But the hope of God's promised Messiah kept her waking up and going through each day.

In just three short and power-packed verses, we get a wealth of insight into the characteristics that marked the heart and life of Anna.

She was a prophetess. In the Bible, we encounter few female prophets, but she was one of them, and her life was marked by prophetic passion. She was eighty-four years old, and we know she had become a widow after seven years of marriage. She exercised significant spiritual discipline through regular fasting, wholehearted worship, and consistent prayer. In a world where women were often quiet in public, Anna spoke freely and boldly to God and people. Let's walk with Anna and be encouraged to feel free to unleash prayers of praise when the Lord shows up in our lives.

READ: LUKE 2:36–38

REFLECT

> *Coming up to them at that very moment, she gave thanks to God and spoke about the child to all who were looking forward to the redemption of Jerusalem.*
>
> **—Luke 2:38**

HER STORY

Who would God invite to the welcome party for his divine Son? The answer, in part, can be found in the second chapter of Luke's Gospel. Besides Mary, Anna was the first woman recorded to have witnessed the incarnation of Immanuel (God with us). What an honor! Like a heavenly spiritual magnet, the heart of Anna was drawn to the temple day after day, week after week, month after month, year after year, decade after decade. This holy place had become so familiar that it was like her home.

Anna knew heartache and loss—all widows do. She was patient and long-suffering. Her eyes may have grown weak with the years, but her spiritual vision was better than 20/20. In her singleness of life and heart, Anna wed together prayer and fasting. Many of God's devoted people through the centuries have done this. Prayer saturated the days and decades as she looked, longed, and waited for the Redeemer of her people to arrive.

When Joseph and Mary brought Jesus into the temple, Anna erupted in prayers of thanksgiving and praise. She approached the couple and their baby son and lavished the infant with prayers of thanks from lips and a heart well practiced for this very moment.

Then came the tiny three-letter word: *all*. Don't miss it. Don't let it slip by. Read the line one more time and catch the gravity of this declaration. After unleashing prayers of thanks and praise, we read that Anna "spoke about the child to *all* who were looking forward to the redemption of Jerusalem" (Luke 2:38, emphasis added). First she prayed for *years*. Next, Anna praised and celebrated when she finally met Jesus. But she did not stop there. Anna lifted up a prophetic proclamation for anyone and everyone who would listen. The Redeemer is here! His name is Jesus!

MY NEED

We all have things we are waiting for. Sometimes we wait for months or years, like Anna did. When we finally see God fulfill the longing of our hearts, two things tend to happen. First, we praise God. Second, we talk about it. When God shows up and proves himself faithful, the best thing we can do is let our hearts and lips erupt with praise.

- What are you waiting for today? Are you doing what Anna did by staying close to God and his people in your time of waiting?

- When God shows up, answers prayer, and fulfills his promises, are you quick to give him praise not only in your heart but also outwardly with your words? Believe God is on the move and practice praise so you are ready to unleash massive worship every time God shows up.

LESSONS FROM ANNA

1. **Persistent prayer pays off.** For decades before Anna met the Messiah, she prayed day after day. Relentlessly consistent and heartfelt prayer floated upward from her heart and lips. Not every prayer is answered in our timing or as we wish. But persistent prayer always pays off, on earth or in heaven and sometimes in both places. For Anna, the fulfillment of her petitions was to meet the Redeemer. What an answer to prayer!
2. **Speak about Jesus.** When Jesus shows up, when we learn who he is, when we experience his redeeming power and touch, we can't keep it to ourselves. We are compelled to give away what we have freely received. For Anna, she saw the Redeemer of her people face to face. Her response should inspire us to do what she did. Speak about Jesus to everyone who is willing to listen.

MY REFLECTIONS

What is God teaching me about prayer through Anna's example?

1. Make a list of some of the people you know who have heard the invitation of Jesus to follow him and have accepted his grace and love. How has Jesus transformed their lives?

2. Anna was moved to tell everyone who would listen about the redeeming power and person of Jesus. Who are people God has placed in your life that need to hear about the saving love and sacrifice of Jesus? How can you share the message of God's love, truth, and presence with these people?

OUR PRAYER

PRAY FOR COURAGE TO SHARE HIS STORY

Write a prayer asking God to give you words and courage to talk with others about the Savior who came to bring us back to himself.

You might want to write out a brief account of the story of Jesus' life, death, and resurrection and how he lovingly offers himself for our sins.

RESPOND BY TELLING HIS STORY

Spend some time in prayer for people you know and love who are still wandering far from Jesus. Ask God to soften their heart to the Savior and pray that the Holy Spirit will give you opportunities to tell *all* these people about Jesus at the right time.

PRAYER ECHOES

From prayers to praise to proclamation—this was Anna's journey. Years of prayer leading up to meeting the Messiah. A burst of thanksgiving and praise when she finally saw Jesus. A practice of proclaiming the message of the Redeemer to anyone and everyone who was willing to hear. Let's learn from Anna and engage in a lifestyle of prayer, praise, and proclamation!

LESSON 21

THE WOMAN WITH AN ISSUE OF BLOOD

Praying for a New Beginning

MARK 5:21–34

HER NEED

MEETING THE WOMAN WITH AN ISSUE OF BLOOD

Her life seemed over. She felt trapped in hopelessness. She needed a fresh start, but the door seemed locked and she had tried every key she could find with no success. What this woman needed was a whole new beginning!

She had been bleeding for at least twelve years. When people have an ailment, sometimes they are known or identified by their illness rather than by their name. Jesus did not define her (or us) by a physical condition. Instead, he called her "Daughter" (Mark 5:34).

Because of the religious and cultural norms of her day, the people would have considered this woman unclean. In the Jewish community, this made her an outcast. She could not enter the temple, come to the synagogue, be near other people, or present herself to Jesus in public. If she did, her presence and condition would make others unclean. She would have felt like a dead woman walking. Her prayer was not just for healing. It was for a whole new life and restoration to community.

READ: MARK 5:21-34

REFLECT

He [Jesus] said to her, "Daughter, your faith has healed you. Go in peace and be freed from your suffering."

–Mark 5:34

HER STORY

"He's the one who has been battling cancer for twenty years." "She's the woman that has had five surgeries, and she's getting ready for another." Many people are known and identified by their physical ailments. It is nothing new. Think about how this woman is spoken of today. She is "the woman with an issue of blood." It is sad when a medical condition becomes a person's identity.

This woman had done her part to find healing. For more than a decade, she had suffered under many medical professionals. She had emptied her bank account and her personal reservoir of hope. After all this, she courageously decided to get close enough to touch Jesus. She would take a risk and see if the power of heaven would be unleashed in her life.

She was physically weak due to continual blood loss. She was considered spiritually unclean, so she was excluded from places of worship. She would have been relationally cut off because of the risk of making others unclean. All the costs of medical treatments crushed her financial world. Her emotional life would have been one of continual discouragement year after year after year.

Maybe the power of Jesus could give her a new life.

As Jesus passed by, she had her opportunity. She believed that the slightest touch of his garment would unleash heavenly healing and restore her broken body, so she reached out and touched the fringe of his garment.

Glory, power, healing, and life were unleashed! She felt it. Jesus felt it. We are still talking about it today.

When Jesus stopped and asked her to identify herself, she responded. Jesus talked to her. She talked to him. Jesus reassured her that the days of suffering were over. Peace was now hers. The faith she exercised unleashed heaven on earth.

In all of this, a nameless woman was given a new name. A forgotten woman was found. A broken woman was healed. The woman who was identified by her illness was now called . . . did you notice? "Daughter!" The Messiah called her "Daughter."

In light of what Jesus called her, let's not refer to her as "The woman with an issue of blood." Let's call her "The one Jesus named Daughter."

MY NEED

Where do you need a new beginning? Are there parts of your life that need a makeover? Draw near to Jesus, reach out, and touch him. Talk with him. Hear him call you daughter. Feel the power of heaven unleashed. It may take time, but don't cease to believe in the one who offers new life every single day.

- Think through your spiritual life, relational life, emotional life—your entire life! Where do you need God to make things new? Reach out and ask for his touch to unleash power in every place you need a makeover.

- Is there a specific area you have asked God to work but have not seen any real change? Bring it to Jesus one more time and ask for him to do a new work in this part of your life.

LESSONS FROM THE WOMAN THAT JESUS NAMED "DAUGHTER"

1. **Persist in faith and prayer.** Never, never, never give up! For more than a decade this woman kept seeking healing, and she finally found it in the Great Physician.

2. **God does his part and we are expected to do ours.** Jesus had the power to heal. He still does. The woman's part was to believe, take a risk, and reach out to the Savior. You and I need to trust Jesus to do his part, but we should never abdicate our part. There is more power in your faith than you know . . . until you reach out and touch Jesus!

3. **What seems impossible to us is always possible for God.** It would have been easy for this hurting woman to give up. Times must have seemed hopeless. Yet, with Jesus, bodies are healed. If you keep reading the entire chapter from today's lesson, you will be reminded that in Jesus, dead bodies rise again.

MY REFLECTIONS

What is God teaching me about prayer through the woman that Jesus named "Daughter"?

1. After twelve years she was still willing to try one more time and reach out to Jesus. What prayer have you given up on and how can you reignite your faith and persistence in prayer for this area of need (in your life or the life of someone you care about)?

2. Why do you think God sometimes waits for us to pray and reach out to him rather than just start fixing things in our lives? How is a divine and human partnership a way for God to grow our faith?

3. If Jesus is never too busy and always available, when are some of the times that we need to lift up our needs to him rather than hold back or wait for the "right time"?

OUR PRAYER

UNLEASH YOUR POWER

Write or speak out a prayer asking Jesus to unleash his power in a situation that seems hopeless and beyond restoration. Do it with bold faith, and see what God does.

"THERE IS NO WAY" PRAYERS

Commit to pray for the big things, the "I don't know if this could happen" prayers and the "There is no way!" prayers. Make a list of some big prayers that you might be a little nervous to lift up:

Big prayer: ______________________________

Big prayer: ______________________________

Big prayer: ______________________________

Big prayer: ______________________________

Commit to pray for one of these every day for the coming week and see what God does.

How God answered one of my big prayers:

PRAYER ECHOES

This woman that Jesus named "Daughter" reached out with deep faith and willingness to cut through the religious red tape of her day. She was in desperate need, so she risked religious rebuke and social embarrassment. Let's set aside proper decorum and tidy prayers. In our deepest places of need and hurt, let's start crying out to God right where we are and reaching out to the Savior when he passes by. And, just for the record, Jesus is always close enough for us to reach out and touch.

LESSON 22

THE SYROPHOENICIAN WOMAN

Bold and Desperate Prayers

MARK 7:24–30;
MATTHEW 15:21–28

HER NEED

MEETING THE SYROPHOENICIAN WOMAN

She was desperate. She needed power greater than her own. Few things move a mama bear more than her child being in danger. This woman, whose name is not recorded in the Bible, was watching her daughter suffer under the torment of demonic attack. She came seeking Jesus because she believed he could set her little girl free. He had the power she needed!

She was a rule breaker. She knew the social and cultural norms, but her daughter was in spiritual bondage, and she was going to get to Jesus and do all she could to ask for his help—even if she came off a bit rude. She was relentless! This woman realized that her power was not enough to set her daughter free, but she would not stop seeking a source of strength greater than herself.

What if there is a source of power great enough to crush the forces of hell and free people in bondage? What if our weakness is not the final word? This woman needed heaven's power and was bold enough to ask. Sometimes desperate prayers spoken from trembling lips can unleash what we need the most.

READ: MARK 7:24–30; MATTHEW 15:21–28

REFLECT

Then Jesus said to her, "Woman, you have great faith! Your request is granted." And her daughter was healed at that moment.

—Matthew 15:28

HER STORY

As is often the case, our story begins with the story of Jesus. As he did on occasion, the Savior stepped away from the crowds and the demands of ministry and found a quiet, off-the-beaten-track place to rest and recharge. This time, he went to a non-Jewish region where most people would not notice or recognize him.

No such luck!

A Greek woman from Syrian Phoenicia saw him, made the connection, and hunted him down. She had heard of his miracles, his ability to drive out demons, and his kindness with strangers, so she dared to break all kinds of social mores. She burst onto the scene and cried out for help, "Lord, Son of David, have mercy on me! My daughter is demon-possessed and suffering terribly" (Matthew 15:22). This desperate mom asked Jesus to show mercy and set her child free.

We would expect Jesus to jump into healing mode and speak words of deliverance. This is not how it played out. Matthew's Gospel tells us that Jesus was silent for a time. It was noticeably awkward because the woman persisted and kept crying out for help (Matthew 15:23). Of course she did. Her little girl was in need, and Jesus had the power to help her.

What comes next could seem confusing to a casual reader who does not know the cultural context and theological underpinnings of what Jesus says. He declares that his first priority and strategic first step in his public ministry was to reach the lost sheep of his own people, the children of Israel. That was his starting point. At a table, you feed your own kids first. You don't start by feeding puppies under the table.

She is not dissuaded. Instead of going away (which is what the disciples wanted), she comes closer. She gets more intimate. This woman kneels right in front of Jesus and asks for help again.

The great Rabbi uses a metaphor that would have been common in the ancient world. As shocking as it could seem to modern sensibilities, the ancient Jews would often refer to Gentiles (non-Jews) as "dogs." Jesus uses this same language, though the New Testament authors depict him softening it by using a diminutive form of the word (little dogs or perhaps puppies). The Rabbi is making a theological and practical point through an illustration. No one would take what the kids need and just toss it to the puppies under the table.

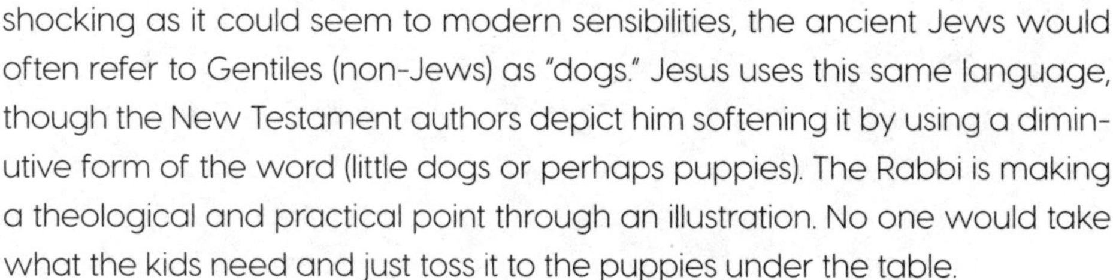

Remember, talking with Jesus is prayer. Asking for the help of our Lord is supplication. This woman is praying, and she won't stop! She responds to the metaphor Jesus is using. When Jesus tells her, "It is not right to toss the children's bread to the dogs," she responds, "Yes, it is!" She disagrees with Jesus! She points out that even the dogs under the table will enjoy the crumbs that fall (and anyone who has ever had a dog knows this is true.). What brilliant and tenacious persistence!

Jesus shifts from Rabbi to the loving Lord of the universe. He praises her for having great faith. The Lord grants her request. At that moment, the demonic spirit leaves her little girl, and she is set free.

Praise God for the persistent prayer of a loving and relentless mother.

MY NEED

There are moments when prayer can't be stopped. We feel so deeply and care so much that we are compelled to cry to God for help. When we pray for someone we love who is in trouble and in profound need, our heart longs to know that God hears and help is near.

- Think of someone in your life who is in bondage: relational, fear, addiction, greed, selfishness, or something else. Let your heart be moved to cry out to Jesus for this person.

- If you are a mother, is there a place of need in the life of a child where you can run to Jesus on their behalf and pray for God's deliverance and help?

LESSONS FROM THE SYROPHOENICIAN WOMAN

1. **Pray with a humble heart and body.** This woman placed herself before the Savior on her knees. This is humility. He is Lord, and a posture of surrendered worship is fitting. Bow your heart and your knees and call on God with a humble heart.

2. **Pray persistently for the people you love.** This mom was relentless and a bit overbearing. The good news is that God loves prayer and welcomes our bold supplications. Don't stop praying for those you care deeply about.

3. **Pray with an expectant heart.** At the end of the day, this tenacious woman's daughter was set free. The enemy was defeated, and the torment ended. This was the dream of a mom who had watched her little girl suffer greatly. Keep your heart expectant while you knock on heaven's door.

MY REFLECTIONS

What is God teaching me about prayer through the Syrophoenician woman?

1. What happens in your heart and body when you actually kneel down and bow before God in prayer? When and where would be a good time for you to be kneeling (if you are physically able) in prayer?

2. Who is a person in your life right now who is suffering greatly in some way, and how could you ramp up your prayer engagement and passion for this person?

3. Can you name a time when you prayed very specifically for a need you cared about, but God seemed to stay silent? How was this prayer answered or not answered, and how did this impact your prayer life?

OUR PRAYER

REKINDLE AN OLD PRAYER

Write or lift up a prayer that you gave up on some time ago. Come back to praying for something you believe God wants to do, but you have not yet seen the results of your prayer.

TRY AN OLD POSTURE

Spend some time praying on your knees this week. You might want to begin each day for one week on your knees. Do this before anything else. You don't need to do this for a long time, but spend a few moments waiting on the Lord and listening for God. This posture is as ancient as the Bible and as modern as today.

PRAYER ECHOES

The Syrophoenician woman boldly came and kept asking even when Jesus was silent. She debated with Jesus like she was a rabbi. She asked again and saw her prayer answered. Hang in there. Be bold and courageous. Don't give up on a prayer that God has stirred in your heart.

LESSON 23

THE WOMAN AT THE WELL

Praying When Everything Is Uncertain

JOHN 4:4–42

HER NEED

MEETING THE WOMAN AT THE WELL

What do you do when everything in life is uncertain? Who do you talk to when your faith is rocked? Where do you turn when you are carrying around a suitcase of questions and a Google search won't provide the answers your heart longs to find?

You would be wise to take a walk with a woman who encountered Jesus and was never the same. We know her by the location where she met Jesus. She was from Samaria, so she would have been someone that Jewish people refused to socialize with. It has been suggested she was an outcast by her own people because of her moral choices. Maybe she faced situations outside her control. Whatever was going on in her life, she came to the well in the heat of the day, and that was a good time to avoid other people. She was empty relationally on that day but full of questions. She was physically and spiritually thirsty, theologically informed and insightful. The "Woman at the Well," as she has been called through history, met Jesus in a moment of intense uncertainty. This led to a prayer conversation that connects with women living with questions and longing for answers.

READ: JOHN 4:4–42

REFLECT

> *Jesus answered her, "If you knew the gift of God and who it is that asks you for a drink, you would have asked him and he would have given you living water."*
>
> **–John 4:10**

HER STORY

She was a woman full of questions.

It appears she had decided to avoid all human contact that day by going to the well at midday in the scorching heat. The scowls, glances, whispers, or outright harsh words of judgment may have driven her from polite society and into lonely isolation, and that is exactly where Jesus met her.

Jesus showed up and broke all social norms. As a man, a rabbi, and a Jew, he had no business talking to a sinful Samaritan woman. When Jesus broke the ice, she responded with a question: "You are a Jew and I am a Samaritan woman. How can you ask me for a drink?" (John 4:9).

Jesus responded to her question with one of the most staggering declarations in all of Scripture. "If you knew the gift of God and who it is that asks you for a drink, you would have asked him and he would have given you living water" (John 4:10). Jesus shifted the conversation from physical water (which she needed) to spiritual water (which she needed even more). The Messiah assured her that if he gave her water, it would satisfy forever.

Jesus taught her that worship is about encountering God in spirit and truth. She went on to (notice the irony) inform Jesus that the coming Messiah would clear up all this worship confusion. Jesus responded with these words: "I, the one speaking to you—I am he" (John 4:26).

Through a series of heartfelt questions and an in-depth conversation (prayer), the woman at the well came to receive Jesus as her Savior. Then, she shared her story with anyone who would listen. This passionate woman explained that Jesus knew everything about her and *still loved her.* She asked them, "Could this be the Messiah?" (John 4:29). She was asking them if they were ready to accept Jesus as their Lord.

The woman at the well came that hot afternoon thirsting for water, but her deeper need was answers. Everything in her life was uncertain. In a conversation with Jesus, she found what she needed most.

MY NEED

If I want to know who wrote a worship song I can't get out of my mind, or the best pumpkin pie recipe, I just type in the first line in a Google search, and the answer pops up. Every question has an answer.

So, why is life so uncertain? Why don't my deepest questions ever have easy answers?

If the woman at the well had an iPhone and typed in, "Why can't I find a man who will really love me?" there would be no satisfying answer. If she Googled, "When will the Messiah arrive?" there might be theories, but they would have been wrong. No one would have guessed that the eternal King of Glory would show up at a city well in Samaria.

What are your questions? What are the things that a computer search can't answer but Jesus can?

Quiet your heart and reflect on these questions. Take time to pray and ask Jesus the Messiah to help you find his answers.

- What are some of the questions that linger quietly in the back of your mind and heart? What are questions that are shouting and demanding you find better answers? (Whisper, "Jesus, help me find your answers.")

- Where do you feel uncertainty in yourself, your faith, other people, human structures, or some other aspect of life? Bring these to Jesus and ask for his wisdom.

As we walk with the woman at the well, we are wise to identify some of the lessons she learned along the way and ask if God might be teaching us some of the same ones.

LESSONS FROM THE WOMAN AT THE WELL

1. **Everyone is invited.** The heart of Jesus is open to all who will come: men and women, Jews and Gentiles, religious folks or irreligious ones. We can come with our questions; he has the answers!

2. **Let go and receive.** Jesus often comes to us and speaks a word to our hearts. The woman at the well wanted physical water, and she wanted to know the place of the right mountain for worship. Jesus gave her eternal water and heaven. That's quite a trade. Is there anything that the Lord has been calling you to give up?

3. **Jesus knows your story.** When Jesus met this woman, he already knew about her former marriages and present situation. He still loved her and wanted to invite this woman into a living relationship with him. In the same way, Jesus knows everything about you, and his love endures. Remember that Jesus loves you where you're at right now.

MY REFLECTIONS

How can lessons from the woman at the well's journey of faith impact my life?

1. Jesus is able to satisfy every longing in our hearts. Where do you need to experience his satisfying provision? Spend a moment in quiet reflection and prayer, being open for the Holy Spirit to reveal and direct the next step in your life.

2. Jesus knows everything about you and still loves you. How does this feel? What are ways you can express your gratitude for his amazing love and grace?

OUR PRAYER

Prayer is conversation with God. When the woman at the well encountered the Savior and talked with him, she was praying. Much of her prayer was asking questions born of her uncertainty . . . and Jesus loved it!

ASK JESUS YOUR QUESTIONS

Questions I am carrying in my heart:

- ____________________
- ____________________
- ____________________
- ____________________

Lift these questions up in prayer. Express these questions and invite God to answer in his timing. Tell God that you will seek to be patient, knowing his wisdom is greater than yours.

DECLARE YOUR TRUST AND CONFIDENCE

The book of Psalms is filled with prayers that include brutally honest questions. Read Psalm 13:1–2. You might want to read it out loud and in a tone that reflects the heart of the psalmist:

How long, Lord? Will you forget me forever?
How long will you hide your face from me?
How long must I wrestle with my thoughts
and day after day have sorrow in my heart?
How long will my enemy triumph over me?

Can you feel the cry of David's heart? He is hurting and has questions, so he asks them to God. He sounds a lot like the woman at the well—honest and bold. The woman at the well ends up declaring her faith and confidence in God. Read how David finishes his prayer in Psalm 13:5–6. Read it out loud a few times, making it your prayer:

But I trust in your unfailing love;
my heart rejoices in your salvation.
I will sing the Lord's praise,
for he has been good to me.

Honesty in prayer honors God. We see it in the woman at the well, we hear it in the cry of David, and this should mark our prayer life. There is no prayer you should hold back. God knows you, loves you, and is waiting for your honest prayers right in the middle of your uncertainty.

PRAYER ECHOES

The woman at the well asked Jesus many questions and had a profound spiritual conversation. Her uncertainty and questions helped lead her to deeper faith. As you walk with her and follow this bold example, may your faith grow deeper than ever before.

LESSON 24

THE ADULTEROUS WOMAN

Praying When You Are Guilty

JOHN 7:53–8:11

HER NEED

MEETING THE ADULTEROUS WOMAN

Grace. Amazing grace. She needed it in buckets.

She was guilty. Caught in the act. Shamed. In need of grace. She is remembered by her sin, not by her name. But like all of us, when she met Jesus, she was defined by the grace of God.

Her cultural and religious setting was one where women could be publicly condemned, judged, and punished for their sins. Notice that she was caught in the act of adultery (John 8:3). When someone is caught in this particular sin, they are *never* alone. But the man was not brought for judgment, only the adulterous woman. This was wrong, but not uncommon in the ancient world.

When we meet this woman, her heart is crying for something she never imagined she could receive: forgiveness and grace. In the presence of Jesus, her greatest need was exposed and met at the same time and in infinite measure.

READ: JOHN 7:53–8:11

REFLECT

> *Jesus straightened up and asked her, "Woman, where are they? Has no one condemned you?" "No one, sir," she said. "Then neither do I condemn you," Jesus declared. "Go now and leave your life of sin."*
>
> **—John 8:10–11**

HER STORY

We meet her just once in the pages of the Scriptures. We know nothing before or after this staggering encounter with the Savior. What we know is that she was caught in the very act of breaking one of the Ten Commandments. This was not a little white lie, or a subtle word of gossip. She was an adulteress.

Imagine you are at church, right in the middle of the sermon. All eyes are on the pastor and all ears are tuned into the sermon. Then, a crowd comes barging in the back door of the church. It is several leaders from other local churches, and they are ushering in a woman who is in tears, disheveled, and ashamed. These religious leaders announce that this woman was caught in sin and deserves punishment. What would this feel like to all those in attendance? Awkward is not strong enough.

This is similar to what happened that morning in one of the temple courtyards in Jerusalem. All eyes were on the great rabbi, Jesus. Then, a crowd busted in, led by a delegation of religious leaders. All eyes would have turned from Jesus to the religious leaders. Every mind would have wondered what was going on.

They made the woman stand in judgment and brought the charge: "Teacher, this woman was caught in the act of adultery" (John 8:4). Every eye would have shifted from the religious leaders to the woman. Judgment, shame, confusion, glances of condemnation piercing as daggers.

The religious leaders continued, "In the Law Moses commanded us to stone such women. Now what do you say?" (John 8:5). We know from the text that this was a set-up, and the religious leaders were trying to trap and accuse Jesus. With all eyes on the Savior, the Pharisees are thinking, *Game, Set, Match. We've got you now!*

What happened next was stunning! Jesus did not answer, but instead he bent down and wrote on the ground in the dirt, and everyone watched him. The Pharisees kept pressing him to give an answer and declare a judgment.

Remember, the woman was still standing there as this was happening. Most likely she was in tears, her eyes fixed on the ground in shame.

Jesus stood up and spoke one simple and world-changing sentence: "Let any one of you who is without sin be the first to throw a stone at her" (John 8:7). Then Jesus bent down and kept writing on the ground. The eyes that were first focused on Jesus, then on the religious leaders, then back on the sinful woman, and then back on Jesus would have turned inward. Every set of eyes in that courtyard would have turned to their own heart, their own past, their own story, their own sin.

We know their eyes went deep into an examination of their own souls because one by one, starting with the oldest members of the crowd, the teachers of the law and the Pharisees all left.

Picture the empty courtyard. There is the woman standing in judgment. There is Jesus, writing on the ground. There are stones on the ground that people dropped when the truthful words of Jesus pierced their hearts and they vacated the temple grounds.

Listen closely and notice what Jesus spoke as he stood face to face with her: "Woman, where are they? Has no one condemned you?" (John 8:10). It is likely that she had not looked up once during this whole encounter. (Would you have?) With tear-filled eyes, she looked around the courtyard, and everyone was gone. Except for her and Jesus. "No one, sir," she replied to Jesus (John 8:11).

Jesus asked a question. She answered. Then Jesus spoke again. This is prayer! Jesus, full of grace and truth, responded to her answer: "Neither do I condemn you . . . . Go now and leave your life of sin" (John 8:11). Grace, grace, amazing grace, and truth: piercing, transformational, unwavering!

This broken woman, caught in the very act, learned what we all discover when we draw near Jesus in prayer. His grace is incomprehensible. His truth is unavoidable. His kindness draws us close, even in our shame. His truth calls us to radical change. His grace is still amazing. His truth is transformational.

MY NEED

Sin never stays secret. Even if no one else finds out, we know, and God knows—that is enough. When our "private sin" becomes public, shame and regret descend, often alongside some private whispers and public condemnation. In these moments we should run to Jesus and not turn away. He is waiting, arms open, to welcome home sinners who have been caught in the act.

- What is hidden in your life that would cause shame and guilt if it became public? Confess it to Jesus now, before it comes to the surface.

- Where is the enemy of your soul pounding you with condemnation and judgment? Run to Jesus and ask for his grace and truth to pierce your heart.

LESSONS FROM THE ADULTEROUS WOMAN

1. **Jesus brings compassion where others condemn.** We live in a world where women feel all kinds of condemnation from others and often from themselves. Judgment about what we do and what we fail to do. Condemnation about how we look and the way we care for our bodies. Guilt over our sin, both public and hidden, and the list goes on. Jesus is the true source of freedom and grace, and he is a new vision of who we are and how God sees us. Remember that Jesus' compassion is bigger than the condemnation of human beings.

2. **Jesus is the bringer of grace and truth.** Some people imagine Jesus as only gracious. They think the Lord is quick to forgive and forget, and that he does not really care about our sin. Others see him as the God who sees all of our sin and can't wait to point it out and bring condemnation. The truth is that Jesus is full of both grace and truth. "Neither do I condemn you"—grace. "Go now and leave your life of sin"—truth. In prayer, we hear words of grace and a heavenly call to repent and follow the ways of Jesus.

3. **In prayer, we discover who Jesus is and who we are.** The woman stood there in judgment, probably in tears. But you know she was listening. Her life hung in the balance of his words. As the Savior spoke, she discovered his wisdom, kindness, and challenging call to change. In the words of Jesus, she heard the grace of heaven and the command to stop sinning. Let your prayer life transform your understanding of Jesus and yourself.

MY REFLECTIONS

What is God teaching me about prayer through the story of the adulterous woman's encounter with Jesus?

1. Jesus came in grace and truth, and we need to do the same. How can you walk in a balance of both grace and truth in the way you see yourself?

2. How can you exercise grace and truth when you interact with people who are controlled by sinful life patterns?

3. Who is a person you know and care about who needs to hear grace-filled words of hope and encouragement? How can you become a conduit of Jesus' tender grace in the life of this person?

OUR PRAYER

NO MORE HIDING

Pray Psalm 32:5–7. Tell God that you are done hiding and ready to lay all of your sin before him. Then, do it!

NO CONDEMNATION

Write a brief and honest prayer about your need for grace. Be sure to declare the cleansing and freedom from condemnation that God has given you through faith in Jesus (Romans 8:1).

PRAYER ECHOES

The woman caught in the act of adultery shows us the tender, truthful nature of our Savior. In her worst moment, she found grace. In her brokenness, she recognized her need for cleansing from sin. As you grow in prayer, be certain that you are drawing near to the God who knows everything about you, who died to wash you clean, and who is ready to lavish you with his amazing grace.

LESSON 25

MARY MAGDALENE

Praying to Be Set Free

LUKE 8:1–2;
JOHN 19:25; 20:11–18

HER NEED

MEETING MARY MAGDALENE

Will I ever be free? Is there a way out of my bondage? Is the power of Jesus enough to break my chains and unleash me from the oppressive attacks of the enemy of my soul? According to Luke's Gospel, Mary had lived with massive demonic possession. Seven distinct evil spiritual beings had residence in her before she was delivered by Jesus. She needed hope for a future, and she found it in the touch of the Messiah.

Mary was from Magdala, a small village on the western shore of the Sea of Galilee.

When she was delivered and became a follower of the Savior, she was deeply devoted to him and the ministry he launched to change the world. Jewish rabbis did not normally have women as public followers, but this Mary seems to have been an exception. Full of gratitude, she became generous toward Jesus, ministering to him all the way to the end. Mary Magdalene was the first witness to the resurrection of Jesus. Interestingly, she is mentioned more times in the four Gospels than many of the twelve disciples.

READ: LUKE 8:1–2; JOHN 19:25; 20:11–18

REFLECT

> *Mary Magdalene went to the disciples with the news: "I have seen the Lord!" And she told them that he had said these things to her.*
>
> **—John 20:18**

HER STORY

Mary Magdalene was possessed not by one demon but by seven. Before she encountered Jesus, she lived under spiritual bondage and attack that few of us could imagine.

Mary received God's extravagant grace, deliverance, power, and love. After she was set free, Mary Magdalene dedicated the rest of her life to serving Jesus. He had broken the bonds of hellish possession and lavished her with amazing grace. In response, she supported Jesus out of her personal resources and helped provide needed finances for his ministry.

When Jesus was arrested, tried, beaten, and crucified, many of his followers pulled back and stayed in the shadows. Mary stood close to her Savior and never left his side. She followed him up the hill of "The Skull" (Golgotha) and was at the foot of the cross as he suffered and died for our sins. Even after Jesus stopped breathing and his heart stopped beating, Mary of Magdala did not

give up on him. Even after they placed him in a garden tomb and rolled a huge stone over the entrance, she stood there crying, waiting, and longing for her Lord.

It was Mary who first encountered Jesus after his resurrection. In a time when the witness of a woman was not accepted in the civic courts, the risen Lord Jesus commissioned Mary to give witness to his resurrection and bring word to the disciples that she had seen the risen and living Lord.

MY NEED

When we realize that Jesus has set us free from the powers of hell, prayer flows naturally. When we look back and think where we could have ended up if it were not for the grace of God, praise erupts in our hearts and on our lips. Like Mary, our life becomes a declaration of gratitude for the goodness of our Lord.

- Where might you be today if you had not been saved by the grace of God?

- Think of a moment when you were so overwhelmed by the goodness of the forgiveness of Jesus that you found praise uncontrollably gushing out of your soul. Ask God for more times like that.

- Remember a time when God set you free from some kind of spiritual bondage and pause to give him heartfelt thanks.

LESSONS FROM MARY MAGDALENE

1. **Jesus has power over the spiritual world and can set people free.** No matter how powerful the enemy might be, Jesus can set us free with a single word. Walk in his freedom and never let the enemy take a place of control in your life again.

2. **Our focal point is not our evil past but our hopeful future.** Too often churches like to tell stories of people who had terrible backgrounds but who have been radically transformed by Jesus. There is something good about seeing the difference Jesus can make in a life, but we should not fixate on past sins and evil. Instead, we are wise to remember the change Jesus has made and focus on where he is taking us for his glory.

3. **Christ is risen, and he draws near his people.** When Jesus arose, he connected with people. He still does. Although our Savior ascended to heaven, we can have a personal and intimate relationship with him every day of our lives *and* for eternity.

MY REFLECTIONS

What is God teaching me about prayer through Mary Magdalene?

1. When was a time you saw the power of the resurrected Jesus set a person free (or maybe you) from spiritual attack or bondage? How did their life change?

2. Why is it important that we focus on the hope and blessings God has planned for our future more than being locked into painful memories of our sinful past? What helps us keep our eyes looking forward and not backward?

3. Mary was given a mission to share what she had seen when she met Jesus in the power of his resurrection. What have you seen Jesus do that you can share with others and inspire them through your Jesus encounter?

OUR PRAYER

PRAISE PRAYER

Meditate on the saving and delivering power of Jesus. Praise him for his sacrifice and willingness to be broken and poured out for you and for his resurrection. Write down a few ways God has set you free and give thanks. God has set me free from . . .

- ______________________________. Thank you, Jesus.
- ______________________________. Thank you, Jesus.
- ______________________________. Thank you, Jesus.

CELEBRATING JESUS WITH YOU

In the next week, make a point of asking one or two Christians you know this question: How has Jesus set you free and delivered you from something? When they share their story, offer to pray, giving thanks for what God has done. Celebrate the saving and delivering power of Jesus.

PRAYER ECHOES

Mary of Magdala spoke with the resurrected Jesus—this is prayer! Begin your day with this simple prayer: "Living Lord Jesus, lead me in the power of your resurrection. Protect me from the enticements of the enemy and give me your power to resist any temptations he puts in my path. Send me on your mission. Help me tell others about you. Fill me with resurrection power this day. Amen!"

LESSON 26

MARTHA

Praying with Bold Honesty

LUKE 10:38–42

HER NEED

MEETING MARTHA

Martha needed to know she could come to Jesus as she was and speak what was on her heart. Could she be honest and transparent and still be loved? Could her personality and temperament be expressed freely in the presence of the Messiah?

She was a truth-teller. She said what was on her mind, even to Jesus the great Rabbi. Martha needed to know that she could speak her mind to the Lord, and so do we.

She lived in the city of Bethany, and her home was a regular stopping place for Jesus and his disciples. She had two siblings that we know of: her sister, Mary, and her brother, Lazarus. Martha and her family were friends of Jesus and had a close connection with the Savior. Maybe that's why she felt so comfortable speaking with raw honesty to the Savior.

Does God welcome us as we are? Will Jesus be patient when we speak our mind? Can we really tell our Maker what is on our mind? Just ask Martha. She did, and what she learned should breathe hope into our hearts.

READ: LUKE 10:38–42

REFLECT

> *But Martha was distracted by all the preparations that had to be made. She came to him and asked, "Lord, don't you care that my sister has left me to do the work by myself? Tell her to help me!"*
>
> **—Luke 10:40**

HER STORY

Since prayer is conversing with God, and Jesus was the Divine One who walked on this earth, every time Martha talked with Jesus, she was praying. Has that ever struck you? When people who lived in the time of Jesus spoke with Jesus, they were engaged in prayer.

One of the most unique characteristics of Martha's prayer interactions with the Savior is that she was clear, bold, and held nothing back.

Knock, knock, knock—someone is at the door letting you know they are there. In the days of Martha, every visitor was a surprise. Remember, there were no text messages, phone calls, or ways to let someone know you were dropping by. Just a knock on the door and company was there. Every guest came unannounced.

On this day, it was a crowd. Jesus and his disciples were standing there, and Martha invited them in. What do you do when a group of people just "pop by"? You start cleaning, cooking, and preparing after the fact. Sounds a bit stressful!

What happens next is humorous and revealing! Martha shifted into hospitality mode. Things to clean. Stuff to be straightened. Food to cook. Have you ever prepared a meal for a group of people or had to clean the house while people were sitting in the living room? But Martha was up to the task. She got to work.

If only she had a sister who was there and could have helped with the last-minute chores. Wait! Mary *was* there. She saw the need. Mary would certainly come to Martha's aid. But there she was, sitting at the feet of Jesus.

This is when we hear the prayer of Martha. "Lord, don't you care that my sister has left me to do the work by myself? Tell her to help me!" (Luke 10:40). Jesus and the guests get to hear what is on Martha's mind.

She does not give a suggestion. Martha directs Jesus, "Tell Mary to help me!" Remember, Jesus was not just a first-century rabbi. Martha was talking with the Lord of the universe.

Prayer is not just us talking to God. It is him speaking to us. When Jesus says, "Martha, Martha" (Luke 10:41), there wasn't a harsh tone or sense of anger. Hear the gentle voice of a parent speaking to a child. Jesus wanted Martha to learn in this tender moment. He was pausing to teach her. She was worried and upset, but he offered peace. She was rushing around while the Lord of the universe was speaking. She was focused on snacks while Jesus was serving a feast. Mary had it right!

In this prayer encounter, Martha boldly told Jesus what was on her mind. She gave him advice. God always wants to hear what is on our hearts with confident honesty. Then, as God often does, he brings the truth. Honest prayer is a catalyst for deep learning. Because she talked with Jesus and declared what was on her mind, Martha got to learn one of the greatest lessons.

Being with Jesus is better than doing stuff for him. It is more important than checking things off a to-do list. Feasting on the bread of heaven is infinitely more important than baking another loaf of bread.

MY NEED

If I speak honestly with God and tell him everything that is on my mind and heart, will he be offended? Am I welcome to pour out my pain, anger, and questions without filters and fear? Can I come like Martha and rant a bit? If these questions run through your mind, walk with Martha and learn that Jesus welcomes your honesty. But be ready for him to be honest with you too.

- When you think about praying with bold honesty, does this make you uncomfortable or does it excite you?

- Since God knows everything, doesn't it make sense to hold nothing back in your prayer life?

LESSONS FROM MARTHA

1. **Talking to and learning from Jesus is essential to our faith.** Martha was responsible and hospitable in doing things for Jesus. These are God-honoring characteristics, and Jesus was not speaking against her commitment to serve. But in affirming Mary, the Savior demonstrated that our first response should be to sit at his feet and learn from him.

2. **We should learn from the healthy example of others.** Sometimes it is hard to learn from the people closest to us (for Martha, it was her sister). Pride can cause us to resent that someone else is doing it right and our need to learn from their example. When God puts someone in our life who is a beautiful picture of faith and following, we should humbly watch and let the Spirit of God shape our heart.

3. **We need to remember that sitting at the feet of Jesus is one of the most important things we will ever do.** Every day of my life offers the opportunity to do many things. Some will seem essential. Others are quite optional. But making time to be in the presence of the one who died to make a way for me to come into the presence of my heavenly Father is always a valuable investment in the flow of my day. Don't let the busyness of life keep you from sitting at Jesus' feet.

MY REFLECTIONS

What is God teaching me about prayer through Martha's conversation with Jesus?

1. What are ways that Jesus knocks on the door of your life and heart? What can get in the way of you throwing the door open and inviting him in?

2. Who is a person God has placed in your life that models bold and confident prayer, and what have you learned from their example?

3. When you take time to "sit at the feet of Jesus," what does this look like in your life? In the seasons where taking time with Jesus is a consistent rhythm, how does this practice bring health, hope, and intimacy with God?

OUR PRAYER

DON'T HOLD BACK!

Write a brief and bold prayer about something that is on your heart. Hold nothing back!

Read your prayer and ask God to help you grow in honesty as you pray. After you lift up this prayer, be silent and allow space for God to speak to you.

SEARCH MY HEART, LORD

Are there things you don't pray about? Do you think such things are too small for God to care about? Too big for God to answer? Too honest for God to handle?

Spend five minutes in prayer asking God to search your heart, and ask him to show you things you need to begin praying about that you have avoided in the past.

I need to start praying about . . .

- ______________________________.
- ______________________________.
- ______________________________.

PRAYER ECHOES

When Martha spoke to Jesus, she said what was on her mind. No reservation. Honest, bold, and passionate prayer. Let her example inspire you to open your heart to the one who already knows what dwells there. When you pray this way, be ready for God to speak back with equal candor and clarity.

LESSON 27

MARY OF BETHANY

Praying at the Feet of Jesus

LUKE 10:38–42;
JOHN 11:28–37

HER NEED

MEETING MARY OF BETHANY

Am I welcome? Must I stand at a distance and feel removed from others and far from God? Mary needed to know that she was invited to come close to Jesus, and so do we. In her day, women were not allowed near a rabbi, but Jesus broke many of the cultural norms.

In two different Gospel passages, we find Mary at the feet of Jesus. One was in a quiet moment listening to her Lord and learning from him. The other was in a time of weeping, deep sorrow, and crying out to Jesus after her brother died. These two very different situations evoked similar postures. Mary came to the feet of Jesus in joy and in sorrow. The longing of her heart was to be close to the Savior. If you want to grow more intimate in prayer and connection with Jesus, walk (or sit) with Mary.

In a moment of joy and in a time of sorrow, Mary needed to know that Jesus would never marginalize her or shoo her away. She needed intimacy with the Savior. Her story reveals that the arms of Jesus are open *all the time*.

READ: LUKE 10:38–42; JOHN 11:28–37

REFLECT

She had a sister called Mary, who sat at the Lord's feet listening to what he said.

–Luke 10:39

When Mary reached the place where Jesus was and saw him, she fell at his feet and said, "Lord, if you had been here, my brother would not have died."

–John 11:32

HER STORY

In Luke's Gospel, we get a powerful picture of Mary at the feet of Jesus. The rabbi had come to town and was staying at Mary's home. In this surprise visit, Jesus was gathered with his disciples and was teaching them. She sat down, right at the feet of the Lord, and opened her heart and ears to his words. She was hungry to learn. She loved being at the feet of the Lord.

Martha felt that Mary was out of line, and she wanted Jesus to set Mary on the correct path. To her surprise, Jesus publicly corrected Martha. With tenderness but crystal-clear words, Jesus let the disgruntled Martha know that

Mary had chosen the better way. In that moment, Jesus clarified the spiritual truth that the best place to be is at his feet.

We also see Mary at the feet of Jesus when he comes to Bethany after her brother Lazarus passed away. Before Jesus entered the city in which she lived, Mary came to the Lord, and the first thing she did was take a familiar posture: She fell at his feet (John 11:32). Once she was there, she talked with Jesus. Mary dared to do what many of us avoid. She mourned, questioned, and unleashed the sorrow that had been locked inside. With a tear-streaked face, she looked up at Jesus and acknowledged that he could have saved her brother. Wow! That is an honest prayer!

Notice what happened next. Jesus felt deeply. He was moved and touched by her tears and the sorrow of those who had gathered. Then Jesus spoke. He did not rebuke her for lacking faith. He did not chastise her for questioning his wisdom. The Savior simply asked a question: "Where have you laid him?" (John 11: 34).

If you know how the story ends, you will recognize that Jesus' question from John 11:34 was the preamble to what he would do next. He was about to raise Lazarus from the dead. With tears in his eyes, Jesus went to the tomb and called Lazarus out. Mary was part of this story, and her prayer to Jesus happened right before Jesus unleashed the resurrection power of heaven.

MY NEED

In a world of pain, rejection, and brokenness, what better place to be than at the feet of Jesus? It is a place of intimacy, safety, and conversation with the Savior. If your heart longs to be near the Savior, learn from Mary and make time to linger at the feet of Jesus as a regular part of your spiritual life.

- What does it look like in your life to spend time at the feet of your Savior? Be creative and try a variety of ways to connect closely with your Lord.

- When is a good time in the flow of your day or week to spend intimate time with Jesus? If you can't find a time, you may be too busy.

LESSONS FROM MARY OF BETHANY

1. **Prayer is relationship.** Prayer, in its simplest form, is about our relationship with Jesus. It is about talking and listening to our Savior. It is being with Jesus, at his feet, walking in the garden, sitting in our prayer chair in the morning, or at any other time and place our Lord meets with us. Be sure to make time for this prayer relationship.

2. **Prayer is listening.** When we have an intimate relationship with Jesus, we will spend time listening. Mary sat at Jesus' feet in her home while others were racing around doing chores. She listened to the great Rabbi and so should we. Prayer is not just telling God what we need and what is on our heart. It is also listening for the still, small voice of his Spirit. Remember to stop and listen for the voice of Jesus.

3. **Come to the feet of Jesus in your sorrow.** Just like Mary, sometimes we experience great loss. We can go to Jesus with our sorrow, and we can talk to him. He can handle our questions. The psalmists modeled going to God in times of lament. Jesus gives an open ear, heart, and door to whatever we want to share. So, pour out your pain and sorrow to him.

MY REFLECTIONS

What is God teaching me about prayer through Mary of Bethany?

1. Where is a place where you meet with Jesus and find a deep connection with your Savior? Why do you think this place is so meaningful to you?

2. Mary listened to Jesus, and so should we. What are ways you seek to listen to Jesus and hear what he wants to say to you? How does the Lord speak to you in the flow of a normal week?

3. When do you set time aside to listen to God speaking to you through Scripture? What are some of the ways God speaks to you through his Word when you read and meditate on it? (Give an example.)

OUR PRAYER

PRAYING FOR BALANCE

Spend some time in prayer confessing where you have invested too much time working for Jesus to the neglect of sitting at his feet. For some, it may also be a time to reflect and spend some time in prayer, confessing that you have spent lots of time at the feet of Jesus learning but have neglected to serve him with the gifts he has given you.

Ask God to teach you a healthy balance of sitting at his feet and receiving from the Holy Spirit and also standing up, going out, and serving Jesus in a world that needs him.

POUR OUT YOUR SORROW

One of the times Mary was at the feet of Jesus was when she faced deep loss. Write out a prayer expressing an area of sorrow you are facing today.

PRAYER ECHOES

Mary felt at home at the feet of Jesus. Consider making time (either figuratively or literally) to get on your knees, flat on your face, or on your back in prayer. Picture yourself humbly placed at the feet of Jesus as you listen, speak, and communicate with your Lord.

LESSON 28

WOMEN IN THE EARLY CHURCH

When Can I Pray?

ACTS 1:1–14;
1 THESSALONIANS 5:17

HER NEED

MEETING THE WOMEN IN THE EARLY CHURCH

Am I welcome to pray? Can I join in with the family of God in this staggering privilege of calling on God? Where can I pray? When can I pray? Are my prayers welcomed and valued? Women in the first century were likely asking all of these questions and more.

Before Jesus came among us, Jewish women were not welcome in many public settings. In the synagogue, they had a very limited voice. When Jesus came, he brought a fresh perspective! Our Savior invited believing and faithful women into his community of followers at a much deeper level. In the Christian community, women had a voice. They were invited into prayer, leadership, and proclamation that their souls needed.

Their names were many. In this lesson, we will learn from a group of faithful, Jesus-loving, risk-taking women. As a group, they are called "women." Yet each had her own story and journey of faith. They were, and still are, the church.

READ: ACTS 1:1–14; 1 THESSALONIANS 5:17

REFLECT

They all joined together constantly in prayer, along with the women and Mary the mother of Jesus, and with his brothers.

–Acts 1:14

HER STORY

Her story is your story. Her story is my story. Women throughout history want to know that their gifts, their voices, and their prayers are welcome in the family of God. As we look at their story, we see our story.

These women had followed Jesus when he walked on the earth as Immanuel, God with us. They had remained faithful to the Lord through his crucifixion, death, resurrection, and ascension. Now the Savior was gone. It was a time of intense persecution of Christians. What would these women do?

They would pray. Faithfully. Relentlessly. In community.

In partnership with the early church leaders they sought the face of God "constantly."

They represented all kinds of people. Jesus drew a dramatically eclectic group of followers. However, they had a number of things in common. All of them loved Jesus, were committed to prayer, had great courage to meet together in a time of serious persecution, and they were all anticipating that something more was coming.

They had seen the beautiful Lamb of God brutalized and crucified. They knew he died, was buried for three days, and rose again. They were aware that he had appeared after his resurrection to many people and had ascended to heaven.

But now, Jesus was gone.

Would things change? Jesus had welcomed women into his closest circle at a time when rabbis did not do this. Jesus had treated them with dignity and invited them to follow him. But would everything go back to the old ways now that Jesus was in heaven?

The words in the first chapter of Acts bring hope and joy. Many of the disciples who had walked closely with Jesus were gathering *constantly* together and were joined by the women who were Jesus' followers as well. Wow! Constant gathering for prayer with women and men together. The work of Jesus was moving forward with the same spirit of unity and connection between all of God's people.

They were living in the spirit of community that the apostle Paul would later describe in his first letter to the Thessalonian Christians, "Rejoice always, *pray continually*, give thanks in all circumstances; for this is God's will for you in Christ Jesus" (1 Thessalonians 5:16–18, emphasis added).

The book of Acts mentions Jesus followers praying thirty-three times in total. That's an average of more than once a chapter. That's what we learn from these women in the book of Acts. They wanted to pray; they were welcome to the throne room of God. Prayer was an honor and a gift.

MY NEED

Is my voice needed? Do my prayers matter? Am I invited into the community of God's people today? Can I learn to pray continually, both on my own and with the family of God? We each need to know that our prayers and praise are just as welcome in the family of faith as they are to the God who calls us to pray at all times.

- How can you join in prayer with God's people in your church and with Christian friends? The best starting point is these three words: "Can we pray?" Ask this often and step into the very throne room of God with other believers.

- When is the best time to pray? The answer is now, in every circumstance, all the time, continually. Think of a time or setting when you rarely pray, and bring conversation with God into this place.

LESSONS FROM THE WOMEN IN THE EARLY CHURCH

1. **Pray in community.** What a beautiful example of gathering to pray in community! Men and women together cry out to God. We have another picture of this in Acts 12:12. There is power in unified prayer. Consider making prayer a priority when you gather with family and friends.

2. **Pray with your eyes wide open.** We are called to pray continually. If we learn to make praying like breathing, part of every aspect of our life, then we will need to pray with our eyes open at times. If this makes you nervous, look to Jesus' example (John 17:1). He prayed with his eyes open, and so can we.

3. **Pray for revival and the fresh work of the Holy Spirit.** We do not have a record of the exact prayers of these men and women who gathered regularly to cry out to God. What we can know historically is that prayer is often a precursor to revival. In this case, the Holy Spirit fell on the church while groups of believers were praying consistently. This should not surprise us.

MY REFLECTIONS

What is God teaching me about prayer through the women of the early church?

1. Who do you pray with on a regular basis? How does this consistent pattern of unified prayer impact these relationships?

2. What are some settings where you can begin praying with your eyes open so you can pray more often? How can keeping your eyes open when you pray (some of the time) lead to greater passion and effectiveness in your prayer life?

3. The early church kept praying (and maybe increased their prayers) during a time of real persecution and oppression. Why is prayer so important and helpful when we are going through hard times? How could other believers support you by praying for you in a hard situation you are facing?

OUR PRAYER

GET A GROUP AND SET A TIME

Designate a regular time to pray with other believers and see what God does through this time. Lift up praise (for what God has done), thanksgiving (for how he has moved), supplication (to ask him to meet needs), confession (for your sins and the sins of your community), and whatever else is on your heart.

GIVE THANKS IN ALL CIRCUMSTANCES

Right after we are exhorted to pray continually in 1 Thessalonians 5, we read that we are to give thanks in all circumstances (notice it did not say "for" but "in"). Write a thank-you prayer to God for being with you in your current life experiences that have been difficult for you.

PRAYER ECHOES

These women prayed consistently and in community with other women and men who loved Jesus. Make community prayer more normal in your life. Look for opportunities in the coming week to say to other believers, "Can we pause for a few minutes and pray together?" You will find unity and deeper community if you make a habit of this. You might even see God begin a revival where you live, work, and worship.

LESSON 29

LYDIA

From Religion to Relationship

ACTS 16:13–15

HER NEED

MEETING LYDIA

We meet Lydia outside the city gates, gathered for prayer with other women. She was religious. She was devoted. She was hungry. But she had not yet embraced the love and grace of Jesus. Lydia was a follower of the Jewish faith, but she had not yet come to embrace Jesus as the Messiah.

In this brief passage, we can identify at least five distinct characteristics that marked the life of Lydia. First, she was spiritually hungry and committed to worshiping God. Second, she was a businesswoman who was successful in her trade. Third, she was humble and teachable and was open to learning about Jesus, the Messiah. Fourth, Lydia had a passionately evangelistic heart. Not only did she embrace Jesus as her saving Messiah, but she also shared her newfound faith with her family, and they followed Jesus and were baptized. Fifth and finally, she was hospitable. Lydia invited Paul and his ministry team to come and stay at her home. What a powerful woman!

READ: ACTS 16:13–15

REFLECT

> *One of those listening was a woman from the city of Thyatira named Lydia, a dealer in purple cloth. She was a worshiper of God. The Lord opened her heart to respond to Paul's message.*
>
> **–Acts 16:14**

HER STORY

Lydia's story is one of prayer. According to Acts 16, she gathered with a group of women by the river just outside of town. This seemed to have been a routine part of her life. She had faith in Yahweh, the God of Israel. So, with devotion, in community with others, she prayed.

On this day, Lydia would learn that the long-awaited Messiah had come to offer salvation and hope to all who placed their faith fully in Jesus. The apostle Paul crashed their prayer meeting. This traveling evangelist had been raised in the Jewish faith and trained by the top rabbis of the day. He had been so serious about his faith that he became a persecutor of the early Jesus movement. Paul had gone on a campaign to destroy churches and lock up people who believed that Jesus was the anointed one.

Once the zealous persecutor encountered the Savior, his life was transformed and turned upside down. After that day, Paul told the story of Jesus everywhere he went. When Lydia heard the message, she believed. She accepted it as the truth. At this point, the Spirit of God moved her heart, and she prayed the ultimate prayer. She made an eternal move from being a religious woman to a follower of Jesus the Messiah.

The ultimate prayer is the moment a person accepts the truth of the gospel. This is the message Lydia would have heard:

- There is a God who made us, knows us, and loves us. (John 3:16; 1 John 4:10)

- We are all rebels condemned to death because of our sin. (Romans 3:23)

- God offered life through the sacrifice of Jesus, the Lamb of God who takes away the sins of the world. (Romans 3:23; 6:23; John 1:29)

- Jesus, the Word of God, had spoken: "Come to me." We respond to his grace by faith alone and say, "Yes, Lord, I come" (Romans 10:9–10). When we confess our sins and declare our trust in him, we are cleansed (1 John 1:9). Then, we take his hand and follow him for the rest of our lives and eternity.

This is the ultimate holy conversation, the most consequential prayer we will ever utter, a prayer to enter into a relationship with Jesus Christ. God calls our name and offers his grace. We confess our sins and declare our faith. When this happens, a lost lamb is found (Luke 15:3–7), a wandering child comes home (Luke 15:11–27), and the angels of heaven rejoice (Luke 15:10). The door is opened, and we have full access to our Father through the work of Jesus as the Holy Spirit leads us. Lydia did this; she received Jesus and so did her family.

This moment launches us into a new life. We can enter God's presence anytime and anywhere. The most holy place has been opened through the sacrifice of Jesus (Hebrews 10:19–22). All obstacles are swept away because of the death and resurrection of Jesus. This was Lydia's new reality. She was a daughter of God through faith in Jesus. Before this prayer Lydia had religion. Now Jesus had her heart.

Have you prayed the ultimate prayer? You might be religious, but have you entered an eternal relationship with the Savior? If you have not, consider praying the ultimate prayer right now.

MY NEED

Have you received the amazing grace of God offered in Jesus alone? If you have, celebrate God's goodness and walk closely with Jesus.

- Lydia had religion, but what she needed was the Messiah. Search your heart and be sure you are not just adhering to religious practices.

- Once Lydia encountered the truth of the gospel, she invited her whole family to hear the story of Jesus as well. Who do you need to tell about the good news of hope, salvation, and new life in Jesus?

LESSONS FROM LYDIA

1. **Start where you are.** Lydia was spiritually hungry. She prayed to Yahweh, the God of the Jewish people. She was on the right track. That's where we all begin: spiritual hunger and curiosity. Wherever you are on your journey of faith, start praying and seeking God. When we seek him, God will meet us where we are and take us to new places of spiritual depth.
2. **Gather weekly with other believers or seekers.** Paul knew where to look for a group of people who were praying. There was a rhythm of Sabbath prayer gathering. We live in a time when weekly gatherings with the family of God have fallen on hard times for many people. Consider ramping up your commitment to meet every week with other believers for community, prayer, worship, and learning from the Scriptures (Hebrews 10:25). If you are part of a local church, make weekly attendance a high priority.
3. **When you hear good news, share it!** Lydia was radically changed by her new relationship with Jesus, and she could not contain her joy. She went home and told her family the same message she had heard from the apostle Paul. What happened was staggering! Her whole family believed, and they were all baptized together.

MY REFLECTIONS

What is God teaching me about prayer through Lydia?

1. Who is a person God has placed in your life who is spiritually curious but not yet a follower of Jesus? How could you encourage this person to begin praying to God in general and Jesus specifically?

2. If you gather weekly to pray with a group of people (not including Sunday worship services), when do you meet, where do you meet, and what happens during this time? If you don't have this rhythm in your life, how could you pioneer a prayer group in the coming weeks?

3. If you have a special prayer place, where is it and what makes it special to you? If you don't, where could you begin praying and how can you make this a sacred place to meet with God on your own or with others?

OUR PRAYER

THE ULTIMATE PRAYER

If you have not done so, lift up the ultimate prayer to accept the grace and love of Jesus as you confess your sins, take his hand, and follow the Savior for the rest of your life and for all eternity.

ADD PRAYER TO YOUR FRIENDSHIPS

Spend some time praying with a small group of Christians in your life. If you have a group of believing friends you connect with regularly but don't really pray together as a regular thing, consider introducing prayer into your time together at your next gathering.

PRAYER ECHOES

Pray for opportunities to tell others about Jesus and be ready to do so when God opens the door. The Holy Spirit might just lead you to a Lydia, who was ready, hungry, and just waiting to meet the Savior.

LESSON 30

WOMEN FROM EVERY TRIBE AND NATION

Praying Now and Forever

REVELATION 5:8–10; 7:9–12

HER NEED

MEETING WOMEN FROM EVERY TRIBE AND NATION

I need to know: Does the God of heaven delight in my praise? My heart longs to be confident that my Maker not only hears my prayers but answers them for his glory and my good. Can I know with confidence that the arms of God and the doors of heaven are wide open to me today, tomorrow, and forever?

Who is the woman asking these piercing and heartfelt questions?

This is the cry of every believing woman throughout history. It is the desire of my heart and yours! It is the longing of women from every tribe, tongue, and people group all over the world. In this lesson, we don't learn from one woman but from multitudes of women who stand before the throne of God in eternity and also from women who still walk on the earth today. This includes you and me.

READ: REVELATION 5:8–10; 7:9–12

REFLECT

And they sang a new song, saying:

"You are worthy to take the scroll
and to open its seals,
because you were slain,
and with your blood you purchased for God
persons from every tribe and language and
people and nation."

—Revelation 5:9

HER STORY

She needs to know that she is loved by the God of the universe and that he welcomes her presence and praise. The longing of her heart is to be confident that this life and world are not the end of the story but the doorway to eternity. Most of the studies in this book are focused on individual women. In this lesson, we hear the songs and prayers of countless women, including you and me.

These women lived in the Old Testament days and cried out to Yahweh with longing and hope. They walked on earth during the time of Jesus, when he was in the flesh and among us. They were worshiping and praying when the church was born, when the Spirit fell like fire from heaven, and when the infant church was first growing up. The women we meet in these passages live in your time, go to your church, and might just live in your home. These women will follow the Savior all the years from today until Jesus comes again. The visions we see in the book of Revelation gather believing women from all times, all places, all cultures, and every language.

These prayers and songs of praise are lifted up from the hearts of every believing woman. They are lifted up in heaven as well as the place you are at this exact moment. They have been lifted up through all time and in every part of the world. The setting of these prayers is where you and I live and where we will live forever.

Do our praises move the heart of God? Yes! Does the God of heaven delight in our prayers? Yes! Is the heart of God open to me and are the doors of heaven swinging wide to welcome me? Yes, yes, and amen!

If only we could see and hear these prayers with our own eyes and ears. In the book of Revelation, we see pictures of heavenly worship and earthly prayers being lifted up to God. Like incense drifting gently to heaven, the prayers of God's people come in every language we can imagine, and some we have never heard. God knows them all and he is listening intently to the prayers of his people.

Through this life, your prayers have pleased God. Your praises have ascended like sweet incense. One day in heaven your voice will mingle with the prayers of countless brothers and sisters and be lifted up in praise and adoration to our God and the Lamb who sits on the throne.

MY NEED

Every woman who has placed faith in Jesus needs a vision of heaven. We need to know that God hears and delights in our prayers. One day this life will come to an end, every tear will be wiped away, every sorrow forgotten, every injustice made right. We need heavenly assurance that this earthly trek leads to glory and eternity in the presence of Jesus.

- When are the times your heart longs for heaven and you need a clear reminder that this life is not the end of the journey but the beginning of something infinitely better?

- Do you believe that God delights in your prayers and praise? Are you confident that the Maker of heaven and earth has prepared a place for you to be so you can be with him forever?

LESSONS FROM THE PRAYERS OF WOMEN FROM EVERY TRIBE AND NATION

1. **Our prayers are like sweet perfume to God.** We have no idea how precious our prayers can be to the heart of God. Have you ever watched a grandparent talking with their very young grandson or granddaughter? The child babbles, tries to form words, and finally says, "I lob yoo." How does the grandparent respond? They don't analyze the words or sharply criticize the child's enunciation. Never! They delight in the intimacy of the moment. When prayer comes from your heart and is lifted to God, he delights!

2. **Our prayers lift up the gospel of Jesus**. In Revelation 5, we hear a prayer song from the hearts of God's people. It is the gospel message—Lamb of God, you are worthy. You laid down your life. Your shed blood paid the price for sinful people. Thank God for the gift of his only Son who willingly died in our place to cleanse us from sin. We will lift up this prayer today and in eternity.
3. **God hears and welcomes men and women from every nation and people group**. Our prayers are lifted to the only true and living God who welcomes everyone who will come to him through his sacrificed Son, Jesus. No national distinctions. No language barriers. No second-class citizens. We will be one family in heaven, so let's start living, loving, and praying with each other now as we prepare for heaven.

MY REFLECTIONS

What is God teaching me about prayer through women from every tribe, people, and nation?

1. Why is the picture of incense such a beautiful image for how we see our prayers and those of God's people through all time?

2. If prayer in heaven will be with people of all tribes, tongues, and nations, how can we begin praying with other believers around our community and world?

3. How does praying the truth of Jesus' life, death, resurrection, and eternal glory bring honor to God and inspiration to us?

OUR PRAYER

PRAYING WITH MY SISTERS

Our prayers are like incense gently ascending to the very throne room of God. Gather with a few Christian sisters for a prayer time. You may want to light some incense or candles and place them where you can see the smoke drifting upward and smell their aroma. Lift up prayers and praises to God. Use the passages from Revelation to guide these prayers, and picture them like sweet incense rising to the heart of God.

- Praise Jesus for how he is worthy of all glory, power, and honor.
- Thank Jesus for the sacrifice of his life to purchase our forgiveness and freedom.
- Glorify God for making us priestly servants and royalty as his children.

PRAYER ECHOES

It has been an honor to walk with you through the journey of learning to pray with the women of the Bible. One day we will gather with all the saints in glory and sing, praise, pray, talk, laugh, and delight in God together. I invite you to pause right now and read this beautiful passage out loud as you close this book, and to keep opening your heart to new vistas and understanding of biblical prayer.

Sherry Harney

Blessing on you in abundance as you grow as a woman of prayer!

> *For this reason I kneel before the Father, from whom every family in heaven and on earth derives its name. I pray that out of his glorious riches he may strengthen you with power through his Spirit in your inner being, so that Christ may dwell in your hearts through faith. And I pray that you, being rooted and established in love, may have power, together with all the Lord's holy people, to grasp how wide and long and high and deep is the love of Christ, and to know this love that surpasses knowledge—that you may be filled to the measure of all the fullness of God.*
>
> *Now to him who is able to do immeasurably more than all we ask or imagine, according to his power that is at work within us, to him be glory in the church and in Christ Jesus throughout all generations, for ever and ever! Amen.*
>
> **—Ephesians 3:14–21**

ABOUT THE AUTHOR

Sherry Harney is the Spiritual Development Director at Shoreline Church in Monterey, California, and the co-founder of Organic Outreach International. For more than three decades, she has spoken about prayer, spiritual formation, leadership, and outreach for local, national, and international organizations. She has also authored several small group study guides and books, including her most recent book, *Organic Prayer: Discover the Presence and Power of God in the Everyday.*